KU-666-924

John Doran was born in Derry in 1930. After leav [...] of fifteen, he served an apprenticeship at a boot and shoe repair shop before joining the Irish Army for a short period. From 1946 to 1949 he was a professional boxer; in 1949 he signed on as a dishwasher with the Union Castle Line and later as a waiter on the Cunard liners *Caronia* and *Queen Mary*. In 1957 he and his family emigrated to Los Angeles, where he worked in the famous Dino's Lodge. Following his return to Derry in 1959, he joined Du Pont, where he worked as a chemical operator and laboratory technician until 1968. From 1968 to 1972 he owned a mobile fish and chip business, and from 1973 to 1988 he was cook supervisor at St Columb's senior boys' college. He still lives in Derry.

To Gerry Hinds

I hope you enjoy this at least half as much as I did writing it

God Bless
John Red Doran
5/3/99

RED DORAN

The Story of a Derryman

John Doran

Illustrated by
Joe Connolly

THE
BLACKSTAFF
PRESS

———

BELFAST

First published in 1996 by
The Blackstaff Press Limited
3 Galway Park, Dundonald, Belfast BT16 0AN, Northern Ireland

© John Doran, 1996
© Illustrations, Joe Connolly, 1996

All rights reserved

Typeset by Paragon Typesetters, Newton-le-Willows, Merseyside

Printed in England by Redwood Books

A CIP catalogue record for this book
is available from the British Library

ISBN 0-85640-573-6

CONTENTS

A BAWLING BUNDLE OF
RED-HAIRED NOISE

I don't know what the weather forecast was on 15 February 1930 but I feel sure from all accounts that it was stormy enough at 5 Fountain Hill, Derry, when I was brought into the world, a bawling bundle of red-haired noise and, I suppose, joy, to an already packed house where the producer was my mother Sarah Ann and the director my father Daniel, shortened to Dan. The rest of the cast were, in line of seniority, Gerard, Mannix, Moira, Terry, Philomena, Sheila, Roisin, Pauline, and

I was christened, I think at this stage for handiness, just John Francis. I was also the last of fourteen, for the first five died at infancy. Now with the stage partly set I would like to take you through different acts and scenarios of my life and share some of my memories I still have from my childhood.

Number 5 Fountain Hill was one of nine terrace houses in a quaint little street about a hundred yards long linking Duke Street to Spencer Road. It sloped upwards from Duke Street at an angle of thirty to forty degrees and joined Spencer Road with a flight of twelve steps the width of the street. Traffic had therefore to enter the street from Duke Street. This flight of steps was my whole world as a toddler and as I grew older the games changed to match the growing agility in getting round the steps. These were unique in so far as hardly any streets had a flight like them and children came from other streets to play on them.

My mother and father married about 1914. My mother had worked in a shirt factory when she was single but after marriage and with the children coming on she became a housewife, that is, taking care of the home and raising a family. My father was a van salesman travelling round the country within a twenty or twenty-five mile radius of Derry, delivering and selling groceries and animal foodstuffs. His job took up many hours a day, so that, since he left for work in the early morning and came home late at night, I did not see a lot of him. At weekends, though, we had him all to ourselves. He was a man of short stature something like myself today and always had a jovial disposition; listening to some of the pranks he got up to both before he got married, aye and after, I don't wonder at some of the antics his sons got up to later. I'm reliably told that he and his pals used to change the signs above business premises at night or at weekends so a butcher might come to open up some morning and find out he had a shoemaker's or tobacconist's sign over his doors or windows. Likewise the other premises would have a change. It caused a wee bit of consternation. I don't know what that would be classed as today but it was good innocent fun then.

He wore a cap during the week but on a Sunday he sported a big black soft felt hat; I think that was the custom then. He was a strong cigarette smoker and by strong I mean the Woodbine or Park Drive – known in their day as 'coffin-nails' – and he would smoke maybe forty to sixty a day. In the end I think this eventually got the better of him. With the hard work and the wettings from the old vans that he was expected to drive round the country in, climbing out and throwing back an old tarpaulin to fish out the deliveries from underneath (there were no big covered lorries in those days with fancy cabs) it was no wonder he died at forty-nine years of age.

I remember my father's van, chain-driven, with celluloid windows and windscreen and a dial on the front of the bonnet to show the temperature of the water round the engine block. We've come a long way from that, eh? My father's death was a great shock to my mother but, on reflection, it shouldn't have been; the signs were there, as he was going downhill for some months before. My brother Terry (now sadly dead) had been 'carrying' him the last year of his life and he only a boy of fifteen or so, still at school. My father bought him an old bike, so that after school he would ride out to a predetermined spot to meet him and help him the rest of the day. That's why he called Terry 'my right-hand man'.

My father was off work only a short time and one night my mother thought his feet were very cold so she asked Terry to lie at the foot of the bed to keep his feet warm. I slept in the next room with Gerard and Mannix, and my sisters had the two bedrooms directly above. It's funny how vivid some things stand out over the years, for on that February morning fifty-nine years ago, I awoke at ten past eight and everybody had slept in. I jumped out of bed, raced as a seven-year-old would do into my mother and father's bedroom and started to shake my father but he wouldn't wake up; so I reached across to my mother and said something like, 'We've all slept in and my father won't waken.' My mother said, 'Don't worry, son. You go and get dressed.' A few minutes later she came into my room to say that my father was dead. He had died during the night; Terry's efforts to keep his feet warm had been in vain. As I said, it was a great shock to my mother for she seemed to be the last to know he was so ill and I often wonder why the doctor in attendance didn't try to prepare her. My mother was forty-eight – not a good time in life for such a blow.

My father was 'waked' the statutory two nights and I was allowed to stay up as long as I wanted. I can see all the clay pipes and cigarettes yet, laid out on the tables as was the custom. The clay pipes had to be specially filled, for there was a knack to it; too tight meant a hot pipe and too loose – well take your pick. I suppose it burned away too quick. In nearly every parish there was a pipe-filling expert who would be called in for the job. By the way, I got loads of clay pipes after everything was over.

Of course this was all away above my head, for my seventh birthday was the following week and it took me a while to realise my father wasn't coming back. Pauline was eight the week after and Roisin ten, Sheila twelve, Philomena fourteen, Terry fifteen, Moira sixteen, Mannix seventeen and Gerard eighteen. The year was 1937 and as my father was the sole earner, things looked bleak. My mother got the widow's pension. I think it was 7s 6d a week for herself and 2s 6d each for Roisin, Pauline and myself – a total of 75p in today's money. It was an insult. My father had worked in the All Cash Stores, a chain of grocery shops throughout the town owned by a Mr Porter and he had a fleet of vans to cater for the outlying districts of Derry. When my father died, all his colleagues at work made a collection and it came to £10 but Mr Porter took it, saying, 'That's a lot of money to give to any woman at one time so I'll put it in the nearest branch shop where she can draw groceries on it until it finishes.' And that's exactly what he did. I can recall going up to the Spencer Road shop where the book was lodged and getting the bread, butter, sugar and flour and the other basics, until the £10 had run out. I can tell you with ten to feed it didn't take very long.

In the meantime Mr Porter, who had stood over my father's corpse and knew his epitaph was 'Honest Dan', couldn't see it in his power to offer any of Honest Dan's sons a job but asked Terry to show the new man my father's route, which he did, without pay. The new man gave him the price of a smoke at the end of the day but Terry earned it, for sugar came in 224 pound bags and flour 140 pound bags and these had to be carried in to wee shops and houses on the route. I can tell you the work wasn't light. Gerard and Mannix both had a similar arrangement with other vanmen in the same firm. Work was scarce in 1937. Moira got a job in one of the shirt factories as a 'clipper'; this was where you started your apprenticeship to the shirt-making, so the wages were very low indeed. Only the other day I saw an actual wages book dating back to 1927 and then the women were being paid less than £1 per week for forty-eight hours; so what could a young girl, just starting the trade, expect?

As I have already said, my father's death was a terrible shock to my mother. She was devastated. Why couldn't somebody have told her he was so ill? She just couldn't get over that and it took her years to go into that room again. I'm saying this, for there was no way that she let us younger ones know how she felt, as she always showed us the sunny side of life. One of her favourite sayings was: 'Laugh and the world laughs with you; cry and you cry alone.' I caught her crying only once and that was when I was married and gone from the house.

Since I lived just around the corner in Duke Street I always called in on passing. This day I called in to say hello and see if she needed anything and there she was sitting in the kitchen in the quietness of the day and I was in the kitchen before she realised it. She hurriedly wiped the tears away while I was bombarding her with questions: 'Who was in? Who annoyed you? Who was it?' But she said, 'Nobody. I was just thinking on the times when I had you all around my knee and I could wipe your noses and I knew where you all were, but now you are all grown up, I wish it could start all over again.'

My mother was small, about five feet two inches, slim of build, and always wore her clothes well. There was no need for make-up, as her skin was beautiful and clear, and her choice of glasses was stylish, rimless. When leaving me to school daily, she would always make me walk proper and swing my arms, 'To keep you warm,' she'd say. She was a Long Tower woman – her father built the house next to the graveyard in Long Tower Street where she was born and reared and where he ran a coal business. He also 'took' land out at Braehead – possibly where I am living now – and grazed cattle. It seems he was very enterprising but unfortunately it did not rub off on any of his family, so when he died and the will was read there was nothing left. A lot of money was owed to him for coal but his customers had a sudden loss of memory; so my grandmother sold up and the sons – my uncles – either joined the army or went to sea. My mother was married at this time, so she was out of the picture but I know from her talk that she was disappointed in them.

As for my father's people, well they didn't bother about us, so we didn't bother about them, for in a way my mother was a Derry woman as opposed to a Waterside woman. I think she was a social outcast. Today that sort of thing doesn't matter, for since the start of the Troubles in 1968 there was a big shift of population from the Derry side of the River Foyle to the Waterside. I should mention here that Derry is both a seaport and a garrison town at the mouth of the Foyle. The river divides the town in two and facing north to the left is Derry and to the right, Waterside. The Derry side are mostly Catholics by birth; Waterside? a mixed bag, Catholics and Protestants. The Waterside people kept to themselves. The place was like a village on its own and the phrase 'over the town' meant going over the bridge to the Derry side.

My mother loved the Long Tower and her favourite stories were of Father Willie Doherty, long since gone, and how he rebuilt the Long Tower – and how he put his hand on the armoured car and all the mechanics in the country couldn't move it until after the 'trouble' was over. The 'trouble' in this case was known as the June riots of 1920 and the police brought in this armoured car to be used against the nationalist population. Father Willie, passing by on his way to say Mass, asked what kind of vehicle it was and the smirky answer from the driver was: 'To shoot boys like you', and Father Willie put his hand on the bonnet and said quietly, 'I don't think that'll do much harm.' Do you know, the ould thing never moved from the spot till the trouble settled days later.

I loved these stories and my mother would relate them to me on my way to school while she was going the same road to nine o'clock Mass every morning in the Long Tower. We parted company at the top of the Dark Lane, named in Phil Coulter's song 'The Town I Loved So Well'; while my mother went down Charlotte Street to the chapel I dragged my feet down Hogg's Folly to an open prison camp called the Brow of the Hill run by the Christian Brothers. I use this term 'Christian' very loosely, for whilst the founders may have had the best ideals, by the time it came our turn 130 years later they were anything

7

but Christian. I dreaded my schooldays, for they were a nightmare. I'll say no more on that subject for now.

My mother liked a snuff and she bought it twopence worth at a time. I can remember running up to Cheshire's wee shop in Spencer Road for Gallaher's snuff (it had to be Gallaher's) and watching the wee woman weighing it out into a wee paper poke she made herself. The weight was a quarter ounce and the scales used were very small with two pans, one for the weights and the other for the snuff. To see Miss Cheshire weighing – none of your computer scales here – was an education in exactness.

My mother, as with the women of her time, stayed at home, where she was always there for us. Looking back, it was a full-time job feeding and clothing nine of us. The big flat scones baked on top of the Stanley range would do your heart good and now and again the 'shop' bread would be bought as a treat. Being left a widow at such an early age and with so large a family doubled her responsibility and whilst there was a lot of love and affection, her word was law. The family were very close and everything has been shared even to the present day. I suppose there wasn't a lot of wealth about, but sure everybody or nearly everybody in the street was in the same boat.

TWELVE STEPS

Now I should mention the street itself, which was known locally as the 'ould hill'. It connected Duke Street to Spencer Road, helped by the aforementioned twelve steps at the top, but sad to say all the houses in Lower Fountain Hill have been pulled down now, along with Duke Street, to make way for a dual carriageway. By the time this had happened I had married, travelled the world, come back and was now resident in Derry for keeps.

I remember the day they were knocking my house down. It

was entirely coincidental that I should be passing on my way to visit my sisters, who at this stage had just been, as the local people would say, 'redeveloped' to another area. It was about 6.30 pm and the light was fading, and as the crane with the huge ball crashed through the front wall and upstairs windows of what was once my whole world; it jolted me back to a world of memories. For as I stood there with my eyes full of tears I could hear all the laughter and crying echoing through the crash of the demolition ball. Within ten or fifteen minutes or so, it was all over and 5 Fountain Hill was history. I stood there for a while in the lamplight thinking of the past and who all had lived in my wee street.

Starting at the top, in the first house under the steps was Louisa. I never knew her other name but she seemed to be old for as long as I could remember, with her hair tied back in a bun and her face wrinkled. She was always very tidy and wore a blue flowered overall apron where she kept her snuffbox and handkerchief in one pocket and her wee money purse in the other. The snuffboxes were all standard amongst these old women – empty Colman's mustard tins – and they were shiny with handling. Louisa never bothered us weans in the street but looking back now I can see her standing at her door watching over us playing on the steps and every so often warning us of the dangers when we got too boisterous. This was before the days of universal radio and television but then Louisa was getting a live show all day, every day. When it came to bedtime and we were all called 'in', Louisa would step into her – was it lonely? – world with nothing but memories of the day past. We didn't look at that side at all – we were too young. She was good, and sad to say she was gone from the door when I came back from one of my trips to sea. She had died and it was only then that I took the bother to discover that her surname was O'Neill. Why did I not know that before? I suppose I felt I knew her well enough as a child for she was always there at the door.

Next door down lived Francey Doran known as Big Francey. He was married to Wee Nana and they had four children – two boys, Herbert and Sammy, and two girls, Susan and Alice. Although the girls were a few years younger than me they sort of took part in our street activities until they found play pals of their own sex. I always thought girls were unnecessary baggage anyway but Herby and Sammy were always part of the gang. Big Francey worked as a stableman-cum-driver for McClafferty's funeral undertaking business and Wee Nana was a Scotswoman, and she was a good wee soul. Naturally she spoke with a Scottish accent and this made her different. Nana was as wee as Francey was big, hence their names. They had the distinction of having a brass nameplate on their door and I think now it had something to do with the funeral undertaker that he worked for.

The houses were really small with a downstairs front room about ten feet by ten and a kitchen living-room. There was no such thing as running water or inside toilets, which in my day were were called lavatories, and these were always situated in the backyard furthest away from the back door. Still coming down the 'hill', as we called it, was Friel's: Wee John and his wife, known just as Mrs Friel to us children. They seemed so old to us and were a lovely couple. Mrs Friel always gave me a poke of sweets every day. Like mother, she wore rimless glasses and dressed in a flowered overall housecoat. She had no bottom teeth so her chin stuck out. She had a lovely kind look about her and never scolded us when we got too noisy which I am sure we often did. She also tied her hair in a bun like Louisa. I would seldom see her out walking except to go to Mass and she dressed in nice but 'old-date' clothes. I think I was her favourite; I liked her a lot.

Her husband John looked like he could have done the part of Darby O'Gill in the Disney film. He was always laughing at something and he laughed very hearty. He wore heavy serge dark suits and sported a watch and chain on his waistcoat. I looked forward to running errands for them. God rest them, they are both dead a long time and I never knew if they had anybody to think about them or maybe say a wee prayer for them. Maybe they don't need anybody's prayers. They were good people.

There were two Mrs Friels in my life; the other one lived round the corner in Duke Street and the entrance to her house was through a solid wooden gateway and up a path into a lovely courtyard. She rented the front of the house to an old fusspot called Mr Latimer who ran it as a very successful grocer's shop. I think this was due to the fact that he wouldn't give you a thick penny for a thin one, he was that miserable. The war broke out in 1939, so he rushed to join the ARP (air raid precautions) and when the air-raid sirens sounded he would rush off with his hard hat, gas mask and his armband. God knows where he went but he always kissed 'muther' goodbye before he left and since there wasn't a lot of kissing going on in my life at that time I wouldn't miss it. It was like going to the pictures.

He lived directly opposite us on our wee hill with his wife and two grown-up daughters and a son who joined the army as an officer, in a flat on the third floor and the only access to this was by a long flight of narrow stairs. You can appreciate it was very inconvenient to answer the door and maddening if it was a hoax. His front door had the only doorbell in the street so it was fair game for 'knick-knock'. Whenever anybody rang, some of the Latimers would put their heads out the window three storeys up and call down 'Who's there?' and after a fictitious name they would open the door by pulling a string from up-stairs. Seems easy enough but who said life was easy? By the time the Latimers came down to the door we were gone.

Back to Mrs Friel in Duke Street. As she was getting on in years she moved out to her son's house and rented her house to my sister Pauline and Eugene McCormick who were just married and they in turn shared the house with Agnes and me when we got married a year later. It was indeed very good of them, for their rent was jacked up because of it and I don't forget that. Before all this happened, as I was growing up, I used to break sticks for Mrs Friel for the fire. One day she took me out to the wee store that Latimer used to keep his paraffin oil in and she pointed to some old boxes she wanted chopped. Now, I should mention at this stage that Mr Latimer had a shopboy working for him called Billy and his brother Alex came into the firm as message-boy-cum-storeman This wee shed was their domain. I pulled down the boxes only to find them full of cigarettes. Plunder! Mrs Friel returned them to the shop and I'm sure there was an investigation but at eleven or twelve I wasn't interested in the outcome. This was wartime and cigarettes were very hard to get, never mind store away in a wee damp shed; my case rests.

Next door down lived Nellie Doran, known as Big Nellie. She was the woman who took over our house whenever there was a sickness or crisis. I used to think she was a big bully but that was an eight-year-old's opinion. In later years, I used tell the one about the married woman in our street chasing after me – I broke her window! That was Big Nellie. There was quite a large family in Nellie's; one of the daughters, Rita, was my godmother and a son John moved to New York in the 1920s, where I met him many years later and he became a second father to me during my time at sea. His home was mine. He lived on Broadway about ten or fifteen miles from Times Square and although he lived in a ten-storey apartment house the neighbourhood was pleasant. It was an old-world New York, the sort that was depicted in the movies of the city at the turn of the century. His wife Kathleen came from the Wood-lands in Ramelton, County Donegal, and my son Ciaran, his wife Rita and son Rudi live there now.

Another son of Big Nellie's was Paddy who went to England and was conscripted into the army while he was studying for the priesthood and when he got demobbed he entered a monastery in Yorkshire. I think his health let him down and he came out but made his home in the monastery as a gardener or general handyman, got married, had a family and to the present day is still alive. He is the last of the line. Big Nellie's husband John was gassed in the 1914–18 war; so she got a pension and the children got a secondary education. They were very lucky in that respect, for secondary education for the working class was pretty well unknown.

I loved standing outside Nellie's door, for there was always a great aroma of Oxo from the stewpot on the hob. Fancy and all as she was, she didn't have a Stanley 8 range like us. Her wee house was the same size as the other three I've just described and it's a puzzlement how such a large family was reared in it. I think they must have eaten in sittings and then hung themselves on hooks up round the walls at bedtime. This kind of living was normal and it's only since we became 'educated' and started to move out of the family home to get our 'own space' that family life started to fall apart. I wish we were back to that time again, for there was togetherness and happiness about.

Next door down lived an old couple: Maggie Morrow and Eugene Lynn. There was nothing wrong with that, however it may sound. I guess my mother knew them as Maggie Morrow and Eugene Lynn before they were married, and that's the way it stayed. Eugene was a barman in Spencer Road; so with the hours in those days we seldom saw him as pubs were open from 10 am to 10 pm. They were an equally nice couple. I used to run their messages too and I had the yearly contract on Palm

Sunday of taking her palms up to twelve o'clock Mass to get blessed. Lucky for me I knew my way to the chapel by instinct for the bunches of palms were so big I was smothered in them. I could have got a part in *Macbeth* when Birnam Wood moved towards Dunsinane. I used to have about six people's palms and when I gave them back there was sure to be a mix up but I always got a couple of pence from each house. Now and again the Elliott boys would try to sneak in on my customers but they were loyal and chased them. You might wonder why the people didn't take up their own palms; well it was like this: palms were blessed only after High Mass on Palm Sunday and the service seemed to go on forever.

Maggie Morrow and Big Nellie used to feed the pigeons every day. This was a daily ritual and the old pigeons would gather up and practically eat out of their hands. I loved running through them to see them flutter up and hear Big Nellie barging. I wasn't alone.

The next house down held an odd couple. We only knew them as the Crying Man and Crying Woman. I believe he was a tailor by trade. They kept to themselves. Next to the Crying Man's was the stables, where six pure black Irish draught horses were kept. I'll come back to those later. Next door to the stables lived Wee Paddy Hegarty who was a brother of Big Nellie's but she wouldn't let him light because he took a bottle; in other words he 'blotted the copy book'. Paddy was a bachelor, king of all he possessed, lived by himself, and looking back now, I suppose he was the envy of everyone. He had an open coal fire that would burn anything, blocks, old boots, coal – or just anything lying about. There were two hobs, one on each side of the fire, and on one of these Paddy had a pot of soup going all day. Everything went into that pot, for he never seemed to finish it and start a new batch; he just kept adding to it. Well, it killed him in the end, God rest his soul.

15

My mother and him got on like a house on fire. I suppose it was because she came from across the bridge like him and they weren't really accepted in the Waterside. Wee Paddy and myself got on great. I was at sea when he died. He was sadly missed on the hill, for he was one of nature's gentlemen. I can still see him rigged out in his old-date cut suit and bowler hat with a wee Charlie Chaplin moustache, only red, and sometimes he wore spats. When as smaller children we would tease him he would let on to make a 'tear' at us (his warcry was 'Holy just God!') and stamp his feet like he was running after us.

WHITE SCARVES AND
BLACK HORSES

Next to Paddy's wee house we come to an enclosed yard where the funeral hearse and carriages were kept. In those days the hearse was horse-drawn and there was something solemn and serene about a funeral, with the two horses stepping lightly almost at a prance along the street and the driver dressed in his long black coat and wrapped in his black leatherette blanket. He always wore a top hat well brushed – I used to do it for him. If the deceased was an unmarried woman a white scarf was tied

around the hat and flowed down the back. The horses themselves knew how to behave, for they picked their steps very
daintily along the streets and their shoes had rubber pads to muf-
fle the sound. They were absolutely beautiful: sixteen hands
high, pure black – not a white hair – groomed every day and
had their hoofs blackened with a mixture of burned car oil and
soot from the fire.

I was lucky, for I had that job too because the undertaker's
yard was next door to my house. Actually there were three
hearses, so let me tell you about them before I move on. They
were huge glass boxes on wheels. The frame was beautiful,
black lacquered with ornamented scrolls of ropes, anchors and
flowers, and the glass sides were inscribed with floral decorations as befits such a solemn occasion. The wheels were finely
spoked and the hub made of brass or in some cases chrome and
they were polished every day. Inside, where the coffin rested,
were chrome rollers to ease its passage in and out, then chrome
stoppers to keep it steady.

This puts me in mind of the story of the funeral going up
Creggan hill: to begin with, this wee man – we'll call him
Wullie – lived in Creggan Street and, poor soul that he was, he
had a hump on his back. Although he was well liked to his face,
behind his back he was known as 'Wee Humpy'. One day he
took a very bad cold and started coughing, but since it was in
the days before penicillin, he died. Now, as was the custom in
those days, the neighbours came into the house and laid out
the corpse and so it was with Wee Wullie. They felt that they
would use a piece of cord to tie him down in the coffin, just
to be sure. During the wake, in came the parish priest to say a
few kind words over Wee Wullie's corpse and he started off by
recalling his handicap and how maybe at times people would be
unkind in their everyday dealings with him, 'And now he is at
peace and so we should all ask him now that he is in heaven to

see it in his heart to forgive us all.' With that a bus passed up the street, the wee house shook as it always did and the cord tying Wee Wullie down slipped. He sprang up in the coffin and everybody, who a few seconds before had been kneeling in tears, rushed for the door. The parish priest was last out and his coat caught on the handle of the door and held him fast. He was scandalously heard to shout: 'Will you let go me coat, you humpy wee bastard, you!' Now, if you think that was bad the funeral had yet to come. As it was going up Creggan hill to the cemetery didn't the horses stumble; the coffin slipped out the back door, slid down the hill and crashed through Eugene O'Hare's chemist window where it burst open and Wee Wullie sat upright again and said to Eugene, 'Could you give me something to stop this coughin'?' Well that's the story as it was told to me!

The harness on the horses was of black leather straps, patent leather collar and straddle, adorned with chrome fixings, buckles and chains. The horses' coats were shining. You know, I think people were actually dying to get a run on the hearse. I was lucky to be living so close to them and I soon installed myself as stableboy. There was no money involved but who would look for money for a dream come true? I know I didn't. At this stage I was about ten years old. The two paid stablemen – they would have called themselves grooms – were John Burnside and Andy Nicholl. John was all right but didn't have a lot of time for children. Children can sense things like that but Andy, known behind his back as Andy Gump, was different, for he had a way with them. He knew a lot about horses too and treated them right; he would never abuse an animal. I thought he was great. As soon as I came home from school at half-three I dumped in my schoolbag under the stairs, hoping maybe not to find it in the morning, and in next door to the horses. They were my whole life. I do believe I smelled like a horse but even my best friends wouldn't tell me about it.

The undertaking business was run by a Derry family by the name of Hill and they also had a furniture factory and retail outlets to go with it both in the Derry side and the Waterside. You could say they were quite well off. Old Jack Hill, I remember, travelled round the town in the pony and trap driven by Wee Paddy Hegarty and it was a quare turnout. If my memories serve me right the harness was of brown leather and the bridle had chrome buckles and ornamental chrome chains. The trap itself was made of brown veneered mahogany with brass handles on the door and a brass step. It was of the kind known in the trade as a 'bucket' trap from its shape and then there were the black leatherette blankets to wrap around your legs. I can tell you it was as good as any Rolls Royce. The rig was stabled over at Mr Hill's home across town but now and again Paddy brought it home with him to work on it.

One time Mr Hill got a new pony, a young unbroken one, and Andy broke it in, assisted by yours truly. I felt like Roy Rogers when I had to take it down Fountain Hill to Duke Street and let it get a taste of the traffic. Boy, could it rise on its hind legs, when the old cars backfired – I think on purpose – and people really did stop and stare; I loved it. Show off!

Next to the stables was my house and as I said at the start, I was the youngest of fourteen but the first five died as infants; the other nine including myself reached adulthood. We were four boys and five girls – what you might call steps of stairs with about a year or so in between. We were very happy and close, and with Pauline, Roisin and myself being the youngest my mother poured all her love and affection onto us when my father died.

Sheila and Moira got a job in the shirt factory and Roisin and Pauline followed them when they were fourteen and old enough to leave school. The shirt and collar trade was the industrial backbone of Derry and there's a lovely bit in 'The

Town I Loved So Well' that goes something like this:

> In the early morn the shirt-factory horn
> Call women from Creggan, the Moor and the Bog,
> While their men on the dole play a mother's role,
> Feed the children and then walk the dog.

My mother paid a Mrs Gregory from Abercorn Road a sum of money she could ill afford to teach my other sister Philomena the dressmaking, as this was the apprenticeship system in those days, and looking back I realise it was nothing more than free labour. According to Philomena, for the first eighteen months there all she did was make the tea and run messages, not for the business, mind you, but foutery things like groceries for the house. Male unemployment was very very high, so in most houses the woman was the breadwinner. Where the man was the breadwinner, however, one of nice things was that the wages at the end of the week were handed over to the head of the house, namely the mother, and she acted as manager, paying off bills and generally keeping a roof over your head. When you handed in your wages, naturally you got something back but you knew that in the middle of the week you would be looking for a hand-out; and you somehow always got it. Very little did you; it took little to entertain you, for it was a great time to be living.

As I have already said, Gerard, Mannix and Terry were working as unpaid unofficial helpers on the vans, so this enabled them to do some trading on their own. There was a thriving pork-processing trade in Derry at this time and Gerard, Mannix and Terry would go to the pork plant or 'store' as it was known, and buy the 'parings' from the bacon, wrap them into two or three pound parcels and sell them, on the side, to the All Cash customers. Mind you these parcels were of good value because the parings, though mostly fat, always had a good piece of lean meat on them. You see, this was before machine cutters or computers dictated how much meat, fat and entrails should come off each carcass.

Between my older sisters and brothers I didn't have to worry about anything and you could say I was spoiled or, at least, cosseted. Life was great and on a Saturday it would have done your heart good to hear my sisters trying to outdo each other (and the Warke girls from round the corner in Duke Street joining in in competition) as they cleaned the windows, inside and outside and upstairs and down, and them singing at the top of their voices all the hits of the movies which was the only top-ten medium in those days. Gracie Fields, Deanna Durbin and Delia Murphy and many others sang round our backyards, for Sheila thought she was Carmen Miranda and Delia Murphy rolled into one. There was singing all the time.

Next door lived the Cregans, Paddy and Sarah with their family Mary, Georgie and Patsy. They were quiet people. Paddy kept a wee donkey and cart and did odd jobs, chopped sticks for the fire and sold them round the doors. It was a living: as I said, very little did you. Paddy sort of growled at you when he said hello and went on about his business and from this you might gather he wasn't a great conversationalist. His wife Sarah seldom came out except to stand at the door and get a wee breath of air about her. She wore the usual floral cross-over apron or housecoat with her grey hair tied back in a bun. She too was a very quiet person and didn't have a lot of friends around the doors, but my mother and she got on well. The boys Patsy and Georgie helped the father, so although they lived next door and were around the same age group it wasn't until they reached their teens that we would have played together. When they grew up they spent a while in the armed forces of His Majesty King George VI, Patsy in the RAF and George in the Royal Navy. The war was coming to a close and I'm wondering now was it their joining up that speeded up the end of hostilities? Their sister Mary married a sailor here in Derry but went off to live in England, where she still lives, although I believe the sailor has died since.

Paddy kept canaries as a hobby and he had as many as thirty or forty about the house; their singing was powerful. On the odd good day he would take some of the cages out to the backyard, where they ran the gauntlet of cats or, deadlier still, the air pistol, which could be rented at three old pence a day, and boy! was it great for shooting seagulls down the quay. When Paddy put his canaries out for air this is where the air gun came into its own, for the canaries became sitting ducks. Needless to say I was too young to rent the weapon but I used to go on the canary or seagull shoot with the older boys.

Next door to Cregan's was Ginny Campbell, who ran a wee paper shop on the corner. God, she was a turn on her own! She went to church on the radio, because on a Sunday when you went in for a newspaper she had the radio on listening to the church service. If you spoke out loud – which we always did for spite – she roared at you. For all that, she was a good spud. She had two sons and two daughters and a husband, Joe. Her son Ronnie was one of our gang and he delivered the *Belfast Telegraph* round the streets in the evenings. Depending on the mood I was in, I would sometimes help him. He had other activities like the scouts and Sunday school and such. In later years he formed a dance band but by then we had grown up and started to cut our own niche in life. Lexie was a year older than Ronnie and he died at about twelve with a ruptured appendix.

That was a bad time for us, for another one of the gang died with tetanus aged ten. We felt that the whole world was closing in and we used to sit at night round John Finn's fire chopping sticks and each of us became experts in afterdeath. All the 'what-would-happens' were discussed. The two daughters were called June and Olive but when they moved I lost touch.

THE BUGGA BOO AND
THE DEMON BARBER

I guess that's the wee street. By the way, there were houses
on only one side; the other was taken up by a huge wholesale
shop that ran up from Duke Street to Spencer Road and it was
here that Mr Latimer lived. He had that whole side of the street
to himself. Goods were brought in by horse and a four-wheeled
flat-top cart and where the horses came in from Spencer Road
there was a yard with a shed in it. It was here the dynamite was
stored for agriculture purposes. I mention this in passing, for my

brothers Gerard and Mannix, along with Nuddy Elliott, Dinny Bryson and one or two others broke in to it and blew it up. There was hell to pay that day; some of them got burns that scarred them for life. They were all about ten years old; so no criminal charges were laid. It was there we fought the war, beat off Indian raids, outwitted the Arabs – anything that was showing at the Midland picture house that week; like Robin Hood, Cochise, Magua, King Kong, Tarzan (we had swings from the billboards). We even had Dracula.

This was all before television. As a matter of fact, radio was quite new too. There was one in our house, powered by a large glass battery full of acid which had to be charged every so often in Johnny Whiteside's garage, which reminds me of how easygoing things were. Johnny had this garage in Duke Street and you had to drive over the footpath to get your car in for repairs and there was a single petrol pump on the street – no special grades in those days – at the edge of the pavement. One day, as he was having a conversation with another man, a car pulled up looking for petrol, so Johnny, busy talking, says, 'Sorry I'm out of petrol. Try So and So's up the street', and just kept on talking. Oh to be able to do that nowadays!

Charlie Jenkins had a shoe-repair shop on the far side of Duke Street. He was an old ex-soldier, at one time stationed in Ebrington Barracks, who married a Derry girl and settled in the town. He was good at his job but very regimental and most of his trade came by way of the army. By 'regimental' I mean he was a great man for time, for he opened the shop every morning at quarter to nine, closed at quarter to one for lunch, opened again at quarter to two and closed at six in the evening. (There was a half-day on Thursday.) His shop was spick and span, unlike the usual cobbler's, with the shelves dusted every day and the whole 'bends' or sides of leather of different weights hanging up neatly arranged along the wall. Years later I had the nerve to open in opposition to him. What I lacked in talent I made up in nerve.

He did competition work, like decorating the soles of shoes with sparables in the shape of roses, horses' heads or anything that took his fancy. I used to think: 'If you got your shoes done like that I'm afraid you'd spend most of your time walking on your hands.' That's the jealous streak in me coming out. Charlie and myself would get into some fierce arguments about England and what she had done to Ireland. I would go back to Brian Boru and relate all his battles. This was from a ten- or twelve-year-old getting it straight from the Christian Brothers that very day, so it was still fresh in my mind. It was almost like the man who just found religion and on hearing how the Jews had crucified Our Lord he proceeded to batter his Jewish neighbour living up the street from him. When the Jew said, 'That was 2,000 years ago', yer man says, 'I only heard about it yesterday.' I know now that Charlie was having me on.

The Elliotts had a blacksmith shop just round the corner and I longed to go in there just to watch but they weren't too sociable – at least they didn't like children about the place. I was fascinated when they were fitting the iron hoops on the cart-wheels, with all the steam and clanging of the hammers and the two or three men tapping the hot hoop into position. I suppose the noise helped for there seemed to be a lot of, 'Right, Nuddy; go ahead, Jack; Paddy, you now', and this sort of banter would go on. It was very exciting for a wee boy of my age. When the heat was on and everybody was engaged in their job I would sneak in to watch and then some smart aleck would relax, turn around, spot you and then shout, 'Come on! Out you go!' and you were thrown out.

Across from the blacksmith was Orlando Cafolla's ice-cream parlour and as small children we were frightened of going in there because of the full-size stuffed brown bear holding a light in its upturned paw and grinning at us with huge fangs. It was certainly terrifying but as I got a bit older, naturally I became a bit more daring, though I still watched the bear out of the corner of my eye, for there was no sense taking chances, eh? Orlando had a couple of billiard tables in the backroom which had a glass roof and this was really out of the ordinary for me because I had never seen one before. Now and again I would sneak in to sit and watch the older boys playing. Cafolla's billiard room was out of bounds to me or my age group, for I always got the story of ill-spent youth from my mother and her word was law. At the end of the day I didn't miss much as there was too much to do outside, like worlds to conquer and battles to be won; so my day was busy enough.

I should point out that Orlando was very temperamental and would fly off the handle for no apparent reason and burst into a whole 'travally' of Italian, to which we had no immediate answer. When you are ten or twelve and can barely speak your own language it's best to sit tight and say nothing. I well remember the day he auctioned the contents of his house and shop. As the place was open to the public, myself and a couple of the gang, average age twelve, made our way up to the attics and there, amongst other things, was Orlando's dress-suit tails, stiff dickey, top hat and cane, the lot. So yours truly put them on and thinking it was just old junk, I started doing Fred Astaire out in the street. At twelve years of age old good clothes are junk.

Heaven was just next door to Cafolla's: Morrison's drapery and toy shop and every year at Christmastime they put on their toy display and with all the lights on it was just fabulous. I took my stand along with the rest of the gang, with arms outstretched to claim all within as mine. Our noses were flattened against the largest windowpanes you ever did see and, come to think of it, I bet there wasn't a handkerchief between us as we pushed and shuffled to claim the most toys as our own. It was a great shop and I loved going in even to ask the time – any excuse was better than none – and watch the overhead rail that took the money and receipts from the counter to the office. It was worked like a slingshot. You never see them any more. Morrison's were away ahead of their time. Old Mr Morrison – he was old to me – was always in the shop and greeted the customers as they came in and made sure that they were being attended to right away. The shopgirls had to be on their toes.

I always got a toy for Christmas – Gerard and Mannix and Terry saw to that – but there was one toy I never got and I used to stand and gaze at it for what seemed hours. It was the centrepiece in the window: a fort with soldiers and cannons and all. I can still see it and I always think no boy should be without one. My mother, God love her, did her best to make it like Christmas but on reflection it mustn't have been much fun for her but she carried on. We were indeed a very happy family.

Next to Morrison's came Harpur's shoe factory and here they made boots and shoes under the Shamrock brand. When the war came civilian orders were put to one side for the duration and army contracts got priority; so they were at it full time. I would like to point out here too that Harpur's had an all-Protestant labour force just as Morrison's labour force were all Catholics. I'll say this for Mr Morrison: he was a man of pride and principle for on VE Day – the day the war ended in Europe – he hung out four or five flags: Union Jack, French tricolour, Norwegian, Russian and a couple of others, including the Irish tricolour. The RUC came and ordered him to pull in the Irish flag, so he took them all in. As the locals in Derry would say, 'Fair play to him!'

Duke Street was a busy street, a real lifeline to the Waterside. Facing Morrison's was an empty lot about two or three houses wide called the Bugga Boo and often gypsies with sideshows would come there. For a small charge you could see their monkeys, Russian ducks, exotic birds and snakes, and you could play roll-a-penny. This is where you rolled an old penny down a little groove to land on a marked-out board with the possibility of winning more pennies. I think the groove was rigged, for I never did see anybody win. Still, the thrill of the gamble was there.

Since there was no water laid on in the site the gypsies depended on the young boys about the district to carry water from their own houses and this guaranteed a free pass in to their show. The war came, and on that vacant ground, the Ministry of Defence built an emergency water tank to be used in case of an air raid. It was to make sure that there would always be a supply of water for fighting fires. The tank was about sixty feet by a hundred feet by ten feet deep and it would have made a great swimming pool except that the water got very stagnant and smelly. We didn't mind, for we used the Faughan to swim in, a local river a couple of miles from town. The Faughan was really paradise and it was here that Tarzan got his comeuppance, for we fought crocodiles, swung from the overhanging trees, and all in our birthday suits. Since no girls were allowed, we had plenty of privacy.

During the war the Yanks come over to Europe to help the British, who at that time were in a pretty bad shape, and their arrival put the Faughan out of bounds for me, because my mother put a ban on it. You see, the Yanks started taking their girls out there and I suppose she didn't want me scandalised. Fair play to her! Another place put out of bounds, officially this time by Dr Farren, the bishop, was St Columb's Park, just newly opened. It was so-named because, as the story had it, the saint had a monastery there and the old ruins were still to be seen. Monastery or no monastery, it became a courting spot, so Bishop Farren in his wisdom barred all his parishioners from going into the park. (In fact these were the ruins of St Brechan's church.) Looking back, there may have been special times in the day when the ban did not apply for some but I know that it was out for me. Anyway, it didn't matter a lot because there were lots and lots of other things to do.

Sammy Scott the 'demon' barber had his tonsorial emporium next to the Bugga Boo and he sported a wee twirled moustache. Although he was my father's cousin we didn't go into it because we were led to believe that, like old Sweeney Todd, he had a lever attached to the barber's chair and when he cut your throat he pulled it, the chair tipped up and you fell down into a cellar where his wife made meat pies and sold them round the doors. That's what we were told anyway so we didn't take any chances. Would you? I think he felt snubbed at not being asked to shave my father's corpse when he died. That was purely an oversight, for the people that came in to wash and dress my father and lay him out on the bed just went ahead and shaved him. I don't think Sammy spoke to my mother afterwards.

On the other side of the Bugga Boo was McCay's, a drab old-date clothes shop that never seemed to be open even when it was. They also had a second shop up Duke Street near the bridge and I think it was the only shop in town to stock Orangemen's outfits, like sashes, black umbrellas and bowler hats. Looking back, I realise that they must have had the monopoly on the gear, for coming near the marching season the shop windows were always dressed up in this stuff.

McDevitt's, a huge drapery and woollen store, was next to McCay's. They sold socks, sweaters and such, of their own manufacture. The McDevitts were wealthy; they had an estate across the river with a drive down to the big house and another drive up, passing the stables and servants' quarters. The house was requisitioned during the war to accommodate the Wrens – not the feathered type but the Women's Royal Naval Service.

The ruins of the house are still to be seen at the Culmore side of the Foyle Bridge.

Before I move on from McDevitt's I would like to tell you a funny wee event that happened in the shop. It was fronted by three plate-glass windows at least fifteen feet by fifteen feet in size and one day a herd of a hundred or so cows were being moved from the train to the slaughterhouse across town and one or two jumped through the window and on into the shop. Well, you can imagine the fun there was beating the cows up and down the shop floor and all the elderly shop assistants up on the counters squealing their heads off and the cowclap everywhere. God, it was great and we really enjoyed it, so much so that we tried to keep the cows in the shop a bit longer.

The same thing happened in Morrison's but the beasts were confined to the window-space. McDevitt's front got a facelift after that and a mirror was installed. We used to mess around with the mirror, standing against it, lifting our legs and arms and it made a really funny effect. It was childish, I know, but years later I saw the comedian Harry Worth use it in one of his television series.

Beside McDevitt's was Stevenson's bread shop which we seemed to ignore, for what reason I can't remember, and next to that John Adams had a saddler's shop. You could spend all day watching him making saddles, bridles and other parts of harness, and he would never send you away. I was fascinated with all this.

Andy Walker's grocery shop was next door to the saddler's. My father worked for him for a time and one night he was ambushed coming up Caw Brae. I should mention that Caw Brae at that time was a formidable test for the old chain-drive truck and coming near the crest, as the old motor was doing its most, the bandits – for there was no talk of politics at the time – struck and several shots hit the van but luckily missed my father as he drove on through. It was the whole talk and the local newspapers ran a story on it. Andy Walker's only concern was: 'Did they get the money?' So my father took the money-bag off his shoulder and threw it at him and walked out. I think that was when he joined the All Cash Stores.

TATTOO JACK AND
OTHER IMPRESSIONS

Just beyond Andy Walker's was Tattoo Jack's, much frequented during the war by sailors. I loved to stand and watch them
having different parts of their bodies tattooed but as this place
was also out of bounds to me I had to be sneaky about it. The
shop had a couple of pinball machines and one with a crane,
where for a penny you could try your luck at grabbing something like a bag of sweets or a bar of chocolate. Tattoo Jack's
wife kept an eye on you all the time as she didn't like you

winning too much. She was all tattoos herself, over her whole body, and so was her daughter; there was a picture of them both in the window in one-piece bathing suits as was the style of the day and you could see they were fully illustrated. They were English sideshow folk and were billed as 'The Tattooed Ladies' but at the age we were, it was regarded as not suitable for us to look at the picture. Sure we couldn't help it if it was in the front of the window for all to see. Country-and-western music played in the shop all the time and this was in the early 1940s, so we were with the times too; I hear a lot of songs today that were big hits in Tattoo Jack's fifty years ago.

Beside Tattoo Jack's was Mrs Cullinane who was a milliner by trade and her shop had a double window with the building painted white with the doors and windows outlined in black. Up on a ledge above the door was a stone figure of a large bird that looked like the German eagle with wings ready for flight. When the war broke out some busybody drew the attention of the authorities to this and there was a request to take it down. Thank God nobody listened at the time and it stayed until the street was taken away in the 1970s. The so-called developers really made a mess of our wee town. Before I leave Mrs Cullinane I should mention that she was a quaint soul; she loved wearing her own creations and it was said that if a woman as much as looked in her windows she would be out like a terrier to pull her into the shop to make a sale. I swear she would have sold me a hat if I took too long to pass the shop window. I used to run the odd message for her.

Beside the millinery was an advertisement hoarding and in behind it was a bookie's shop, illegal, of course, and raided every turn about. I think the police tipped them off before the raid and some of the punters would take the rap. That kept the courts happy and the police were seen to be doing their job. Maggy Cregan's fruit and vegetable shop was close by. Maggy was Georgie and Patsy's aunt and she was a spinster. Her bachelor brother Micky, or Louten as he was better known, lived with her and to keep him off the street she let him have the big front room upstairs for a billiard table, so it became known as Louten Cregan's billiard room. Every now and again Louten would go on the drink and it was quite a usual occurrence to be sitting with a black over the middle pocket ready to clinch the frame and have Louten barge in like a raging bull. He would clear the table and throw everybody out on the street. He was priceless. I remember one day he was washing the windows for Maggy. Picture two tall shop windows, one each side of the door, and Louten with the long-handled brush scrubbing away. He decided that he had come to the end of the brush work and leaving it against the wall proceeded to throw the remainder of water up round the glass, not realising that his nephew Patsy had dropped a big stone into it. After the crash he cursed a bucketful all right. Patsy had a cousin called Willie Hogan and he was reared with his Aunt Maggy, so we nick-named him 'Dates' because there was always a huge block of dates about three feet by three feet sitting on the counter and they were sold by the penny worth. Maggy was very enterprising, so she kept the family all right for a few pounds a week. She donated the beautiful sanctuary lamp to St Columba's, the Waterside church, and it hangs there still.

Going on down from Cregan's was Eaton's bakery and it would do your heart good to go there in the morning and smell the aroma of fresh baked bread. Their Chester breads were fabulous and it wasn't until I got into the catering business that I really found out how or what they were made of – all the sweepings-up from the bakery floors. Still, you know the old saying: 'Clean meat never fattened a pig' – or something like that. Mrs Eaton was a nice wee woman but I can recall one morning going down for half a dozen German buns and her correcting me, saying that the German bun was no longer the German bun, it was now the Paris bun, just because Hitler had invaded France. So you see: Hitler had an effect on my life as well! The bread was sold round the streets and delivered to houses. The main means of transport was by horse and a special breadcart, where the driver sat up on top, almost like a hearse driver. Sad to say these gave way to small electric vans and the streets were full of them delivering milk and bread. In the mornings the whirr of the milk deliveries woke you up and later on you heard the bread vans.

Across the street from Eaton's bakery were a couple of pubs and then coming up towards the hill again was Ernie Rossen, the 'Whispering Man' who ran a bicycle repair shop and also hired out the heavy upright cycles we called 'bedsteads'. During the 1920 troubles someone left in a 'flying bedstead' for repair but forgot to tell him that there were explosives in the hollow crossbar. When Ernie started to saw it, it exploded and he lost his voice, hence the nickname. Strangers going in would be taken aback when he would whisper to them and some would look all around and whisper back. I think this made him mad.

A man called Johnny Curran ran a music shop where records could be bought or rented and since we had a gramophone my father used to send down regular and rent the latest John McCormack or whatever. He loved 'Your Granny Has Left You Her Old Armchair' and 'Abdallah Bulbul Ameer', both sung by Frank Crummit. When war broke out Johnny Curran went to Belfast and his shop became a vegetable shop, then a tearoom, then a fresh fish shop and then it closed its doors for good.

There were a couple of coal yards in the street but the main one for me was Lane's, relocated but still going strong today, and it was here we got our weekly coal. When the coal boats from England, Wales or Scotland came in, the coal was all

36

worked by hand and drawn away from the quay to the yards or depots by horse and cart. A docker had his work cut out for him in those days, for it was pure slavery getting into a hold full of coal to start digging down through to the bottom. They were paid by the day and no matter how much money they got I'm sure it wasn't enough, God bless them. Looking back now, it was an awesome sight to see this gang of men coming up Duke Street with their coal shovels slung over their necks. Some of them had two shovels, of different shapes, one for digging down from the top and the other for digging at the bottom, where I'm sure it got easier. After a day's work these men were pure black with coal dust and only the whites of their eyes and the red of the insides of their mouths showed. Needless to say there were plenty of pubs in Duke Street and the pubs got the most of their pay. My mother used to say that this was Saint Columcille's curse on the Derry dockers.

Cochrane's Row angled off from Duke Street down to Lane's coal yard and there was a row of seven houses down one side. In the evening after six o'clock when the carting stopped this was our football pitch and anything else we wanted it to be. Now and again when we would get too boisterous and noisy Martha O'Neill or old Mrs Hannigan would tell us to clear off. This happened several times a day, so we got used to it. We would weather the storm by moving on down the street a bit and then work our way back.

Further up Duke Street towards the bridge was Cafolla's fish-and-chip parlour where you could also get ice cream – the best in Derry – and one of the attractions there was the slot machine which could be 'fixed' with the right touch. Dan Marcini was a partner of Mrs Cafolla's and I think she died shortly before the war, so this left Dan running the place. He was exactly what you would see nowadays advertising ravioli or spumoni or some such Italian dish with a waxed moustache and a cook's hat, flat and floppy on top. He would spring out from nowhere just as you were getting a few pennies from the machine, grab you by the scruff of the neck and give you a good slap round the ears. Boys, he was rough, and during all this he would curse away in Italian. I know he was cursing, for you couldn't speak nice in thon tone of voice. The funny thing about it was, when you went in to buy chips he was nice as pie, so civil; how people can change, eh!

Dan married a local woman and had two sons, Freddy and Josie, but the dead Mrs Cafolla had a son and daughter in England and after the war they came home to claim their inheritance. In the meantime Dan had died and now Freddy and Josie were out on the street. Maybe there was more to it than that but that's how it ended up. Archie Cassoni, another Italian, came along and bought out the young Cafollas and he ran a very successful café until the whole street was gutted out and turned into the dual carriageway.

Across the street from Cafolla's was the Broadway Bar, still in existence at time of writing, and next door was Reid's butcher shop, alas gone now and replaced by Lewis Fastravel agency. Kelly's chemist came next and it was a treat to step into this old-fashioned chemist shop in the times when the chemist himself made up most of the medicines, pills and rubs, and would give you a quick diagnosis on the side. During the war when sweets were rationed I used to buy Ovaltine tablets and eat them like sweets and Kelly's kept me supplied. Old Mr Kelly would look at you over his – to us – funny shaped glasses. The medicine bottles came in all different shapes and colours: clear, blue, purple, green and amber, each one suited to the medicine prescribed and every transaction was recorded by hand on the paper roller on the till. It was bookkeeping at its best.

McCay's who sold the Orangemen's regalia was next and then the Oval Bar, where later in life I used to 'stand in' for the barman John Nicell on his night off. Next door was Lynch's paper shop, which had a handbell attached to the upper inside of the door, so as you entered the bell would clang and old Mr Lynch would shuffle out from the back kitchen. By the time he got to the counter with his game leg and stick we would have run away. I know you are thinking it was cruel but sure I never pretended life was any other way. Mrs Selfridge had a fish-and-chip shop next to Lynch's but her chips didn't taste as good as Cafolla's. Next to Selfridge's was Adair's grocery shop but I didn't have much truck with them, so I'll give it a pass. Next to that was an empty shop which my brother Terry took over just to live in the flat above. Finding a house was desperate in those days.

Coming on down the street we had Thompson's Seed Store, which was a large wholesale and retail outlet for farming implements, seeds and animal foodstuffs. It was a real thriving business but still retained the old-world style of wooden floors and a lot of their goods were kept in drawers with the name of the particular item beautifully painted on the front. They kept everything you could imagine. Then there was Malseed's, an equally big store that wholesaled groceries to smaller shops and it took up the whole side of Fountain Hill fronting onto Duke Street. Because I lived so close to it, I guess from an early age I felt it was mine and the men working there would have given me anything I wanted, like wrapping paper, cords, rope and wood for the fire, simple things nowadays but much appreciated when I was growing up.

That about sums up the great big world that I started out my life in but thanks to the devil planners it's almost all gone now, making way for a wider highway to a bigger traffic jam. Nothing lives for ever.

THE YANKS
ARE COMING

Duke Street, though the busiest street in the Waterside, was really only about a quarter of a mile long, running from Craigavon Bridge to the LMS railway station. The continuation of the street was called Bonds Hill and this took you to the Ebrington Army Barracks where in my day, pre-1939, the South Wales Borders where billeted. I can recall watching the officers riding out to the hunt, mostly on Sunday mornings, with twenty or thirty dogs – beagles I think they were – running behind. It was a quare sight indeed as they rode down Bonds Hill up Duke Street and out of sight either over the bridge or up the Prehen Road. You could see a lot of time was spent on the grooming of the animals but this was peacetime and the soldiers had nothing else to do. About sixty or seventy of them paraded to church on Sunday for 10.30 Mass. I'm not sure now if they had reserved seats or not but after Mass they would assemble outside the church on Chapel Road and do their wee drill. This consisted of shuffling their feet and touching the man on their right; then on the command 'Right turn and by the left quick march!' they would stamp down Chapel Road just in time to join in with their Protestant comrades coming out of Clooney Church. Then they would all go home together.

The war was actually declared on Sunday 3 September 1939, and the whole world changed. Derry was shook out of its tranquillity and all of a sudden forces in uniform were all over the place. I was nine years old. A lot of the Protestant people rushed to join the Home Guard (a bit like the earlier Territorials) and later made famous as 'Dad's Army'. They were kitted out in soldiers' uniforms and trained to shoot – not a very hard job since most of them were already well versed in that field, being members of the B Specials, an auxiliary branch of the Royal Ulster Constabulary. The majority of the Catholic population didn't even bother to join because it was England's fight – so let her get on with it. However, a big number of Irish Catholics did fight and die in that war, for these were the people that had to go away from home because there were no jobs, and rough it in England on construction work. Then when the war was declared they were conscripted if they had been working there for two years. Some joined because there was nothing else for them to do, no work and worst of all no prospects. And others joined because they wanted to fight Hitler. These men joined regular regiments like the Inniskillings (known as the 'Skins') or the Royal Ulster Rifles, and a lot of them lost their lives at Dunkirk.

Most members of local branch of the Territorials had joined to defend Ulster and home to the last, but not all. Some Catholics had been members since the Munich Crisis in 1938, joining to supplement their pay with the weekend stipend. They found themselves in action far from home, thanks to Rommel, the Desert Fox. The Germans had run riot all through Europe and now Rommel was scourging North Africa. So who to send to stop him but Sir Basil McFarland and his bunch of Royal Artillery Terriers? I must say that as an eleven-year-old who had never seen an army march off to war before, except in the movies, this indeed was a very exciting day. I can see it yet: the train at the platform, some carriage doors open and soldiers and women crying and all that kissing and hugging. It was pathetic, nothing like the movies, no stiff upper lips here, I can tell you. One of the soldiers even ate a bar of soap so that he would froth at the mouth and be allowed to stay. While all this was going on some girl fancying herself as Gracie Fields started to sing, 'Wish Me Luck As You Wave Me Goodbye'. The train's whistle blew and slowly it puffed out of the station, the men destined for somewhere in North Africa. And as the saying goes, 'The band played and we all walked away.' All I can add to this is that there couldn't have been a lot of fighting done, for pictures soon appeared in the local papers of the soldiers celebrating the Twelfths of July and August in the deserts of Egypt. I'm sure that big sphinx must have been disgusted looking down her broken nose at them. Watching them and their wee parades, she was probably thinking, 'Little amuses the innocent.'

The quays that up to now only had taken coal boats were hastily modified; the river was dredged or deepened to handle much larger warships like corvettes and minesweepers, and the

English soldiers that we were once used to in our streets were now replaced by foreign sailors like the Free French, Norwegian, Dutch, Russian, Polish. Derry, owing to its geographical position, was strategically placed as a base for the minesweepers that protected from German submarines the armaments and food convoys from America to England and Russia. The U-boats patrolled a radius of about 400 miles, so though the ships were safe far out at sea, as they approached land, their worries would start.

With the rest of my family, I witnessed, while on holidays at the Isle of Doagh, a British ship getting blitzed off Malin Head by two German dive bombers. It was on a Sunday morning and that afternoon the ship limped for asylum into Buncrana, in what had been Éire since 1937 but which we still called the Free State. What was so strange was that two Irish planes flew past and didn't bother to engage in the fracas. I think this was because the Irish Premier de Valera declared Éire a neutral state.

Hitler's armies were having spectacular successes in Europe: Belgium, Holland, Norway and France – not necessarily in that order – had fallen and the British retreated to Dunkirk, a little seaside place on the coast of France where one of the great miracles of the war was performed. As news of the retreat reached England every little boat that could float put to sea and sailed for Dunkirk where they picked these soldiers literally off the beach and ferried them out to bigger ships that couldn't come close enough. This was one of England's finest hours, even if she would say so herself.

Derry wasn't quiet for very long because the Yanks arrived to set up bases for the invasion of Europe. We didn't know it then but that was the long-term plan. The Japs bombed Pearl Harbor in Hawaii which brought the Americans into the war and one day we awoke to the sounds of a lot of American civilians coming up Duke Street from the railway station. Some were dressed as cowboys with holsters and guns slung at their waist, cowboy boots, chaps and big hats and others wore check shirts like lumberjacks. I had never seen a real live American before let alone a cowboy, and on top of that I had never seen so many big men. It was a great exciting time in my life. Their job was to build the camps for the fighting forces to follow. They threw us children fistfuls of money and I scrambled as good as the rest. There were chocolates and chewing gum which was all brand new to us – even before sweet-rationing our chewing gum looked different – and some of them started to shoot their guns in the air but looking back now I think they may have been using blanks, for I didn't see anybody fall.

Watching old Pathé newsreels of the war in Europe, I could identify with the people of the wee towns in France and Italy as the Yanks started to liberate them, for that was how they behaved with us that first day in Duke Street. The only difference was: this mob were civilians. Some of the Royal Navy were still in Derry and although they were supposed to be allies somehow the Yanks didn't like them, so naturally the fights started and on that particular night in Duke Street it was like a scene from the Barbary Coast. I myself had a ringside seat down Mill Street when a Yank squeezed a wee sailor to death in a bear hug and then threw him away from him like a ragdoll. He was a very big man, possibly twenty-four stone, and the sailor a normal ten or twelve stone, a perfect mismatch if ever I saw one. I still see that big hunk in my mind being led away by his buddies to Ebrington Barracks and story has it he went back to Sing Sing where he came out of.

The story also going the rounds at the time was that when America was so rudely pulled into the war on that infamous day in December 1941 a lot of the prisoners in jails throughout the States got an offer they couldn't refuse: help the war effort or stay in prison; so I'll leave it to your own imagination. This is a verse from a parody on the US marines' march 'The Halls Of Montezuma'.

> From the halls of Montezuma to the huts at old
>   Springtown
> You can see them in their uniforms go marching up
>   and down.
> First they took them out of Sing Sing and dressed
>   them up in green;
> Then they sent them here to Derry as United States
>   marines.

Well, wherever they came from they were welcome, for the local boys got working again and a bit of dignity to go with it. For just about that time the IRA had a bombing campaign going on in England and internment was imposed here in Ireland, both in the Six Counties and the Free State. The country was in a terrible state for here in the north if you had nationalist tendencies at all you were in danger of being interned in Crumlin Road jail in Belfast under the Special Powers Act. By this means a lot of innocent young men and women where incarcerated until the end of the war. There was also the 'forgotten' ones who were barred from employment in public works – war work and such – and these men, while not interned, had the word 'suspect' stamped across their claim in the Labour Exchange.

This is fact, for my three brothers Gerard, Mannix and Terry and a couple of their friends had this happen to them. Mannix was digging with a pick and shovel at the construction of the airfield, where the Du Pont company is now, when he was marched off by an armed guard of B-men as a terribly high security risk. Terry, a lad of sixteen years of age, got a job as an apprentice engineer and my mother was elated; it was like getting an 'ology' nowadays. The only thing was, it didn't last long, for on the same day he too was marched off Derry docks as black as hell with soot from a ship's boiler. He was classed an even higher security risk. Gerard at this stage had already said, 'Hump you', or whatever the vernacular was in those days and went on to greater things like smuggling and making fun of His Majesty's Customs. It was good while it lasted, for all during the war he enjoyed himself and made a lot of money.

At this time in the Free State there was an 'emergency', so de Valera had a form of internment in the Curragh army camp and I am reliably told by a soldier who was there at the time that the Irish troops weren't easy on their own kin. Harshness and deprivation was expected from the RUC and the B-men but somehow it didn't work out like that for they seemed a wee bit more humane.

It seems like I'm drifting but I'm only clearing the way to see the picture of my wee town at the time of my growing up. I am now eleven years of age and apart from the odd image of the Derry terriers holding the Twelfth in Egypt, the war was a long way away. There was rationing but with my brothers going out through the country in the All Cash Stores vans we got ample food. The rationing didn't bother my family too much. Anyway it was laughable, for the customs restrictions were more relaxed and half the population of Derry headed across the border every Sunday and picked up whatever they couldn't get in Derry. We had a strict blackout too but it was all lights a mile away in the 'State' because they were neutral. Laughable wasn't it?

The Yanks didn't ask a man what his creed was. If he could do the work he was hired, as quick as that, and if he couldn't, he was fired equally as quick. It seemed a fair enough system but whilst the pay was good the Yank wanted his pound of flesh also. This puts me in mind of a story: a navvy is sent for to come to the site office where the Yankee foreman pays him off. The navvy says indignantly, 'What's this for? Sure I done nothing', and the foreman replied, 'Yeah, I know, look at the picture in your cards.' Sure enough, there it was: a photo of him leaning on his shovel sleeping. No argument there, case closed.

The biggest mechanical crane the town had known came with the Yanks, and the driver, known as Leo the Yank, originally came from Dublin. I would like to say now that he wasn't an ex-con, for he had a successful construction business in New York. Anyway, whenever he had to move this crane from one end of the town to the other, the whole place got so disrupted, for overhead wires had to be cut or lifted and with the narrow streets it was hectic. On top of all this, a great big Alsatian dog like Rin Tin Tin, sat out on the very end of the jib. I think now on reflection the dog was a big show-off but at the time it was great. Leo the Yank married a Waterside girl and took her to America after the war as a GI bride. They stayed for a number of years, before retiring back to Dublin where Leo has since died.

A great number of Yanks married Derry girls and when the war ended and the GIs had gone home the American government arranged for their brides to travel to America on the *Queen Mary* and the *Queen Elizabeth* – it was in all the newsreels – and although that is over forty years ago I still meet the odd one coming home on vacation. Some made it all right, whilst some had it rough. For instance, there was a girl I knew married a fellow from Brooklyn and whatever sort of a yarn he told her in Derry about back home she got a rude awakening on arrival at Pier 90, New York; there on the dock, amidst all the hustle and bustle of wives meeting their husbands, some with war wounds and such, was your man with, not a bouquet of flowers, but a barrow full. The girl said, 'Darling, you shouldn't have got so many; sure a bunch would have done', and he says in his best Brooklyn accent, 'Shaddap, get your hat and coat off, and start selling before this crowd breaks up.' I think in the end it worked out all right for I've seen her back in Derry a couple of times over the years.

There was another girl who lived round the corner from me and she was being pestered by the soldiers calling at her house; so a guard of two marines were put outside her house twenty-four hours a day and she finished up marrying the sergeant. Some said he was Frank Sinatra's cousin because he was Italian and the name sounded the same, but who knows? The name Sinatra amongst Italians might be like Doherty or McLaughlin in Derry, where we are up to our oxters in them. When I started my own travels her father asked me to look her up and gave me her address in New York. I talked to her on the phone but did not meet her. She never came back to Derry and I'm told since that she has died.

Then there was the girl I knew from the Waterside who, wanting to impress her Yank, who said he came from Alabama, invited him to tea one evening, and to put on a show she blackened her sister's face and tried to pass her off as a black maid. You see, a good steady Yank was a quare catch at the time, as he was a source of silk stockings, candies and foodstuff and such. By the way, this girl lived in a wee two-up two-down terraced house, so there wasn't a lot of room for entertainment; unless she told the fellow that the mansion was being done up and they had just moved to the gate-lodge.

In the blackout you could have said anything. 'Blackout' simply meant just that: no lights shown at all. Each house had to have special curtains and if even a slightest chink of light got out you were liable to be reported by maybe your neighbour in the ARP and have to pay a severe fine. The few cars that were running had to have special hoods with slits over their headlamps and at night you had to move around by sound. It was really bad and the laughable thing about it was, as I have mentioned, that a mile or two across the border the lights blazed away to the heavens. This invisible border ran through Pettigo on the Donegal/Fermanagh border so that one side of the street was blacked out and the other side was lit up. Did you ever hear such nonsense!

Well, back to the Yanks. My sister Roisin's pal, Teda Doherty, had a sister Aggie who married a Yank and he rode around the town in a Harley Davidson with a sidecar. I think he must have been some kind of a cop because he carried a gun slung low like a cowboy with a badge like the American cops wear on his belt. I remember going into the house one day and Aggie's younger brother Paddy had the old granny in a corner pleading with him to give her the gun that he was pointing at her. I was about twelve and he about seven or eight. The Yank used to leave the gun and holster hanging over the nearest chair and go to bed. I would say the old gran was lucky that day for the gun was loaded.

The first Yanks, the technicians, were a mixed bag of civilian tradesmen and, as I have already said, they came in advance of the troops to build their camps. In the Pacific the Japs give them such a rough time that these technicians were recalled and trained in the art of warfare, given a uniform and a rifle and so became the Fighting Seabees – from the initials of Construction Battalion. Trust the Americans.

During all this time the River Foyle was packed with the smaller kinds of warships, corvettes and destroyers and minesweepers. There were also merchant ships gathering up for convoy possibly to Murmansk. These convoys were in terrible danger, for the German U-boats worked in packs and exacted a very high price, and many a young sailor would have passed you on his way down Duke Street never to come back. It was indeed sad. Different nationalities came and went and though I was too young to go over the bridge to check I'm sure they had much the same story to tell along Foyle Street.

The Free State's state of emergency was not surprising, since both England and Germany had their eye on it. The Free State had natural coastal inlets where ships could shelter. That was the English interest but the Germans also looked at Ireland as a stepping stone to England. It would be nice to invade a wee country like ours, and I'm sure they would have got a lot of misguided backing from certain factions in this country – to many Irish nationals England was the enemy – but, thank God, it didn't come to that. Hindsight makes clear that it would have been a lot worse under German control; think of Bergen–Belsen and all.

This all leads me up to the first day the American marines came to Ireland. Wherever they came from I don't know but all of a sudden there was a convoy of trucks (it used to be 'lorries' but the Yanks changed that to 'trucks') full of marines dressed in – you'll never guess – green. Now, this was the colour of the Free State troops but the similarity stopped there. While the Free State uniform was of rough woollen material, the Yanks wore tailored gaberdine. At the time people could only see green, so as they made their way down Duke Street and up Bonds Hill to the barracks, many thought we had been invaded by Free State troops and they were met with some cheers. The cheering soon quietened when the big white star appeared on the side of the trucks. Many years later in America I met an old fellow who had been on that convoy and he regaled me with stories of his time in 'Londonderry'. He talked too about the great welcome he got that day on arrival but I hadn't the heart to tell him the people thought it was the Free State troops come to liberate us.

Gerard started work as a truck driver and this was just up his alley for he was nuts about cars and up to the outbreak of war, motor vehicles were thin on the ground. Every now and again he would pass down Duke Street and depending on what he as carrying he would throw out fruit and candies – we were all calling them candies by now – to us along the street. By the way, his smuggling activities were still going on, even to the extent of using one of the American trucks for a 'run'. He was as game as a pheasant. I remember one night he was called out on duty and along with a lot of other drivers, sworn to secrecy. They had to report to Lisahally docks to pick up scores of living and dead American soldiers who were injured at sea off Malin Head or thereabouts when one of the American ships in a convoy with the *Queen Mary* crossed her bows and was cut in half like a tomato. Imagine 83,000 tons travelling at thirty-odd miles an hour hitting 25,000 or so tons right in the middle. The men worked all that night ferrying the dead and dying to hospitals and morgues. We didn't hear of the tragedy for a long time after the war.

Growing up during the war meant that you had lots of good crack when the older boys, like my brothers, and Shan Orr, Paddy, Rory, Nuddy Elliott, Charlie Bryson, Georgie and Patsy Cregan, Seamus O'Neill, the three O'Donnells, Pat, Mick and Edmond, Stevie 'Pigeon' Hannigan gathered to chat. Dinny Bryson regaled us with tall yarns of him being torpedoed off Malin Head and the U-boat commander recognising him and apologising. We would gather around Charlie Jenkins's window in the evenings and stories would be told, brags made about who could do this and who couldn't do that. Then a sing-song would nudge the yarns out of the way and a singing competition would start between Shan Orr and Pigeon Hannigan, though Pigeon didn't have the tone of Shan. Pigeon got his nom de plume from the fact that he believed he could talk to pigeons which he did at every hand's turn. He had a turn in his eye but it didn't stop him from pegging stones, for as the saying goes, he could knock a 'flay' off a mare's arse at 200 yards. He really was a dab hand with a stone.

Georgie Cregan was a character too. He joined the navy in the latter years of the war and one time while home on leave he went into Thompson's for a packet of cigarettes and Thompson said he had none. That was all right, for cigarettes were often scarce, but later that evening Georgie was saying this to Charlie Bryson, and Bryson, whether taking a hand out of Georgie or not, told him he saw Thompson giving cigarettes to a sailor earlier in the day. My bould Georgie walked straight up the street and put a brick through Thompson's window. The window was at least fifteen feet by twelve feet and old Mosey, that was Thompson's name, came out and Georgie said all excited, 'I saw them. There were two of them, Yanks; they ran up the street and over the bridge. Here, I'll help you to board it up till the morning.' Mosey gave him a couple of packs of fags and thanked him very much.

Thompson's was run and owned by Mosey and his brother John. I'll not say they were bigots, but they certainly did not employ Catholics, so we never bothered about them. The big store is still there but they are gone, as is Malseed's. They too had the same attitude towards Catholics, for on Twelfths of July and August it really stood out. For all this, I had a way with the men in Malseed's and try as they would to make me curse the pope, I stuck to my faith, for I knew from my Christian Brothers teaching that as soon as I would deny my faith I would be struck dead on the spot; so I used to curse the king instead. They used to try all sorts of coaxing, like giving me sweets, which in those days of rationing were like gold dust. But sure, looking back now, wasn't I the quare eejit too, for then they would get me to sing all the rebel songs to them and I know now they were taking a hand out of me.

At the end of hostilities in Europe, known as VE Day and then Japan, VJ Day, the main bulk of the Yanks were pulled out of Northern Ireland, so the camps were being closed down.

The camp in Derry at the junction of Strand Road, Culmore Road and Buncrana Road was the scene of an unusual happening. This camp, which was once the shipyard, was the marshalling yard for the American transport – trucks, diggers, cranes, buses and jeeps. When the Yanks started to pull out, one of the drivers was told to take the vehicle home with him and next day the local RUC confiscated it as part of the British war effort. They claimed that it was part theirs and maybe it was, but the Yanks didn't agree with that. They got the men to put all the vehicles in a heap and proceeded to attack them from all sides with bulldozers. They said, 'Hell, those Limeys haven't paid for the damn things and we ain't giving them to them. If you can't have them, well nobody will', so they were all smashed in a heap, as was all the office furniture.

By this time the Americans were well ensconced in Derry and sympathised with the Derry people and their nationalism. They set up a radio link between Washington and London and any messages between the two powers would pass through Derry. The time President Kennedy was shot in Dallas we in Derry had it before London. Something to brag about, eh! The radio station was known locally as the 'base' and it was in operation for almost twenty-five years after the war ended, during which time a big number of the American personnel married Derry girls – aye, and some even stayed here and settled down. I said 'American personnel' because local civilians were employed there as cooks and bartenders and riggers for their aerials. There was a great variety of work and your politics or religion weren't questioned.

THE SLATE HOUSE

In the summer I was the envy of all my pals, for I had six weeks' holidays in Donegal. My mother had some relations in the Isle of Doagh and I can assure you it was better than 'dough'! I mean money, for it was unspoiled. There were no tourists about the place except for the locals returning home on holiday from England or Scotland but this added to the excitement for there were plenty of 'big nights' or parties. My mother had been going there for years before I was born, so she would have been classed almost as a local. The Isle people, as we called them, lived close to the land and depended on it for anything they needed. It was typical of the old Irish way of life on farms which were small but able to sustain a family, and while the work was hard the people somehow seemed happier. In my lifetime I have seen things change only for the worse, for people are not as content now, always looking at far-off fields.

I saw the Isle at its best time, I suppose – in the summer. Then the hay was being saved, the corn and barley harvested and turf cut, turned and brought home from the 'moss'. Yes, it was all go but still there was time to have a big night in our house or someone else's every evening. There were two lovely little beaches, quite safe, walks and a wee bit of hill-climbing. It was real primitive, for we slept on 'tick' mattresses filled with straw and sometimes if we had visitors who stayed over, extra straw was just shook out on the floor for their beds; but sure after a day working in the fields (or should I say 'carrying on'?) we would have slept on a razor blade. We spent the whole summer vacation there, as school would close one day and we would be in the Isle the next.

The big bread hamper measuring four feet by three feet and two feet deep, which was kept up on the attic landing all year, was brought downstairs and the packing started. The hamper was stuffed with clothes, blankets and such, pots and pans; really everything we could think of. Then Paddy Cregan was engaged to take it across the bridge in his wee donkey and cart to the Lough Swilly Railway, where it was put on the train and left at Rashenny station. It was then picked up by anybody passing and left in our house where the door was always on the latch; nobody bothered about locks in those days. The station was four miles away, so it was a godsend to get the old, overstuffed hamper lifted and deposited at the Slate House.

Shortly after the outbreak of war the line from Buncrana to Carndonagh was closed down – a crime! – and the bus completed that part of the journey. As it did not go right in to the Isle, the bulging monster was dropped off at the end of the Isle road. Anyone from the Isle with a horse and cart who was passing knew who it was for and took it the rest of the way. What a lovely caring time to have lived in. It seems haphazard but I can assure you that the hamper was absolutely safe enough, for everybody knew it was the Dorans'.

Horse and cart was the mode of transport in those days; there was only one car in the Isle which came out only on Sundays for going to Mass, whilst the rest of the week it was in the car house. Seems odd calling it a car house – what else? you might ask – but the car house was really for the jaunting car and the cart. The man who owned the motorcar – I don't know what make it was – was called Willy the Shore but amongst our family he was known as the 'Bitching Truth', for everything he said, to him, was the bitching truth and most sentences started with, 'To tell you the bitching truth...' He married late in life – you know, when the old bones were well knit – and lo and behold his 'young' wife died and he started looking around again at some of his old fancies, but one day he 'checked out' and left a fortune. Some young buck from America got it all: land, house, money – the lot. I can see him now driving his Cadillac down some highway in the States humming 'The Hills Of Donegal' to himself, wondering where on under God Donegal is.

We stayed the whole six weeks in the Isle. Looking back, I now realise it was tough on my mother, for although she had few enough amenities at home – no mains water at all – at least she had running water from the standpipe out in the backyard. On the Isle she had to walk over the fields to a well for a bucket of water. Toilet facilities were nil and the everyday washing – and with our family I'm sure there was plenty – was done in a big zinc bath and I can see her yet hanging out the washing on the hedge. When she brought it in she also brought in a few earwigs, or as the Isle people called them 'gulye glegans'. I was terrified of them, for I was told that they could get into your brain through your ear-hole, thus the name earwig. Still, it was heaven, for from as early as I can remember, as soon as we landed at the Slate House the shoes came off and they were put aside for Sunday Mass. This was in keeping with the practice of the rest of the Isle children and younger teenagers, for bare feet was the custom.

My mother had a fear of water, so I had to wait a year or two to try the beaches but I had lots of other things to do. The spuds were already planted and the corn and barley and flax sown but the turf had yet to be cut and 'won'. This is where I came in to my own, for I thought at the time I was a key man . . . getting up at daybreak and yoking up Paddy Dagley's or maybe Willy Owny Brien's horse and cart, whichever took my fancy, and heading up to the moss to work the turf and bring a load home. The horse was the usual heavy-duty farm horse and the cart a wooden box with heavy spoke wheels encircled with iron hoops. There were no springs on this type of cart and as the roads were topped with seashore gravel the going was rough on the bum. The only comfort you had was a hessian bag filled with straw to sit on. I may have had the reins in my hand but looking back now I realise I was only kidding myself that I was driving, for the old horse knew itself where it was going and, I might add, paced itself very well, for no matter how I shouted or coaxed it, it just plodded on at its own speed. It was a heck of a lot smarter than me.

All the same, in my imagination I was heading up a wagon train to Kansas or some such place every trip I took, for there were always other carts on the road and as we went along more horses and carts joined in, all bent on the same mission, for it was the season for the turf. I shot many a Red Indian on the way but, funny thing, they must have collected the bodies, for I never passed any coming home. Going up to the moss could be quicker than coming home because with the tide out we could cut across the strand but the return trip, if the tide had come in, was three miles longer. This journey was done twice a day.

On the days when I didn't go to the moss I worked at the hay and when it came to harvesting time the corn and barley had to be sheafed and stooked, the flax pulled and stooked and the hay cut, turned and ricked. I can't think of anything better than being out in the fields working like this and then the woman of the house coming out with the tea in the tin can and the scone bread well smeared with her own freshly made butter and homemade blackcurrant or gooseberry jam . . . Boy were we ready for it!

It's strange, but I can't remember wet weather. I'm sure there was a fair share of it but my memory won't let me remember it. At night then the Isle people would all gather in to our house and we would have one of our big nights. Years later I worked on the biggest, most luxurious ships that ever floated and in the Statler Hilton in Los Angeles but they never could stand up to the Isle. Happiness and contentment are a state of mind.

The Slate House I remember with great affection. It was called that just because it had slates on the roof, whilst the other houses had thatch. It was the centre point of the Isle, so it was a great gathering spot for the locals. To give you an example of how central it was, during the 'emergency' the army used it on manoeuvres while I was on my summer holidays. The Free State also had an auxiliary force, called the Local Defence Force or LDF, and to back them up was a second force known as the Local Security Force or LSF. Most of the men from the Isle of Doagh joined the LSF, for it seemed you could stay at home and do all your fighting there. It was a laugh at night watching these fellows train with sticks as rifles and them dressed in dungarees and hobnail boots. After a good *céilí* in our house they would line up outside, do a few drills, step on each other's feet and then march off home. The series *Dad's Army* on television had nothing on them.

To get back to the Slate House: some smart aleck in Dublin decided to test his men under fire, so they set up this war game making the house a stronghold or position to be held at all costs and who do you think they nominated or 'ordered' to hold it but the LDF and the LSF. They pitted regular soldiers against them. Came the day and our house and surrounds were packed with big men playing soldiers and there they were, lying on their bellies all about the place keeping a lookout for the 'enemy'. It looked real serious with their wooden guns, for there weren't enough real ones to go round. Anyway, about dinner time my mother puts on a big pot of poundies and scallions and started dishing them out to the 'troops'. All you could hear was, 'Ah Christ Sarah! sure you shouldn't have bothered', and at the same time they'd eat the hand off you. The crack was good and the poundies equally as good, for it made the lookouts forget their mission, and lo and behold the position was overrun by the 'dervishes' and captured. It was a day of infamy, for they blamed Sarah for setting them up. All you could hear that night when they gathered for the usual dancing was: 'Ah jay, Sarah, you lost the war on us!'

The locals would gather into the house at night and tell stories and sing; someone would produce a button-keyed melodeon and there would be dancing, lancers, sets and sixteen-hand reels; and my mother would have an oven scone baked, as big as a cart wheel – slight exaggeration there. There would also be a big three-legged pot hanging on the crook over the fire full of freshly dug, freshly boiled spuds, like balls of flour, just ready to be lifted off and turned out on the creel in the middle of the floor and then set up on top of the empty pot. Round the pot were seats or stools, and bowls of buttermilk were available for everybody in the house. It was sheer magic the way she did it. People didn't visit, they '*céilí-ed*'. Now, the highlight of the night for me was going out in the morning – now that's Irish – and 'finding' all the things that the people left for us, like sacks of potatoes and fresh vegetables, milk, eggs, butter, cans of small fish like fresh sardines – lovely boiled in milk – all left outside the door as the *céilí*-ers came in. Although my mother must have had a fair idea, it was always a complete mystery to me as to who left them.

You could say that we lived very cheap but it was a show of the high regard the locals had for my mother, for our house in Fountain Hill was always an open house or more like a halfway house to all from the Isle. This may seem funny when you think of it but in the thirties and forties transport was a lot slower – oh, to be back in those days – and a visit to Derry took all day; so our house was a great break for them. They could get a bite to eat, go to the toilet, and if they were smuggling, our house was great for taking the contraband off your person for a while. I mind Susy McColgan used to make poteen and she brought it to Derry and sold it to some pub owner who in turn mixed it with Irish whiskey to colour it and the Yanks were crazy about it. The poteen probably knocked them crazy. She carried it under her clothes, so it was handy to have a place like ours to rearrange things. I must make it clear that not everybody who came to our house did that. There were those travelling on to England, Scotland and even America and of course there were those coming home. My mother made them all feel at home.

We had our funny situations too: Dan O'Donnell was bringing a horse from the Isle to Limavady, so he had to pass through Derry and since he had to walk this distance, about forty-odd miles, he naturally rode the horse. When he arrived in Derry he was just in time to head the Orange parade over Craigavon

Bridge with the old horse. It had never heard a band in its life and it was bucking and jumping all over the place; the marchers, thinking it was some fellow doing an impersonation of King Billy himself, cheered him on. The parade passed the foot of my street and Dan was just about able to break off and nearly brought the parade with him, for on a day like that, what with all the old Lambeg drums beating and the blood well boiled up, they would march anywhere. Well, he stopped at our front door and all this time the horse was going mad bucking and lepping, so Gerard said to Dan in jest, 'Bring it in to the house', and, believe it or not, that's just what he did. He brought the big bloody horse into the hall and tied it to the hallstand with all the coats still on it.

There was an air of innocence about the Isle people then but I would feel a stranger in it today, for now they are too sophisticated. When you look back to the ways they used to greet you and some of their sayings, you realise that these are things unheard of now. A typical encounter would sound something like this: going into somebody's house or maybe meeting him along the road it would be: 'How'er ye Paddy?' and Paddy would stand off a bit and then say, 'Aahera jekers, John. Is it yerself! Aahera Christ, ye haven't changed a bit! Aahera, is it down in this part of the country ye are now! Sure there's many a change here since I saw you last.' You don't hear that sort of talk nowadays. Terry and myself met Peter Oggy (young Peter) one day and the conversation went something like this: 'How'er you Peter?' Now Peter was a lean man about six feet four inches, so he was well above our five feet four inches and about seventy years of age to our teens. Anyway he stops and then bends down to our height with his hands on his knobbly knees with the trousers tied with straw rope at the 'anklers', as he called them, and looking at us for recognition before he spoke – maybe the old lamps were dimming – and after what seemed ages I spoke out and said, 'Peter, it's us: John and Terry Doran.' Well he took off! 'Aahera Christ! Aahera jekers, is it yourselves! Aahera, sure it's good to see yous! How are yous doing?' So we told him, 'All right', and asked him how he was doing. He replied, after a good sucking in of breath, 'Not so good.' So we said, 'God we're sorry to hear that. What's wrong with you?' – ask a stupid question!– and he said, 'Well it's like this: when I want to pish, I canna pish but when I do pish, I pish like a hoss.' How can you sympathise and keep your face straight after a statement like that? He was quite serious. But that wasn't it all, for the best had yet to come . . . He nodded over our heads at the house behind us which we knew very well and naming the woman who owned it, he said, 'But I'm not as bad as—there, for the doctor had to come on Monday last and draw the dung from her.' Now, that was how it was said and the man was not trying to be a wise guy or a smart aleck; it was just the best way he knew to describe it.

Such people have all gone now, more's the pity. Blame it on television and radio. Speaking of radio, in my time there was only one radio set in the Isle and it belonged to Johnny Block – a young lad who lived next door to us and although he had a farm of land he didn't work it. I think his father was in America years before he died and left Johnny enough money to keep him. It was a wet-battery set and it was from it that I heard the news that was to change the world for ever. That was the first use of the atomic bomb in one of the deserts of America – and it was used again on the living people of Japan. Roosevelt and Truman have a lot to answer for. It was a short four years later I had first-hand knowledge of the devastation in both Nagasaki and Hiroshima when I sailed out to Japan on a world cruise. It is well-documented, so I won't bore you with descriptions, only to say that I realised looking at the wastage that we humans are the only species on this earth that can think up better ways to exterminate our own kind.

Before I leave the Isle for a while anyway, I should mention that I slept in anybody's house I felt like at the time and I was treated like one of the family. It was a 'Kitty-the-Hare' situation and my mother knew I was safe enough – besides it was always one less to feed. I loved sleeping in the cupboard bed alongside the fire. This was a bed about shoulder high off the floor and it had a sliding door on it and to get into it you had to use a chair or stool. When you got in, the door was slid across and it was like sleeping in a box. A generation before this would have kept a sow pig, as it was coming near to having its litter under that bed and after all the piglets were born and the old sow was feeling better, maybe a couple of days later, they were then transferred out to the pig house. This was for the convenience of the farmer, as he could lie in bed and see that the farrowing progressed all right instead of sitting out in an old pig sty in the cold of the night. By the way, pigs nearly always farrow at night, at least mine did. I feel I am just skimming over this part of my life, for I could go on and on and on. It was like a fairy tale.

Everyone in the family helped my mother as much as she allowed us to and I never heard her complain, for children were her life, but I'm sure she had many lonely days without the companionship of my father. They are both in heaven now, I know. The Isle and that setup was part of my growing up and I can only look back with many very happy memories and no regrets at all. I may come back to the Isle with one or two wee stories later: like the time a mine was washed up on the beach and one of the Dinerias found it and started to screw at it. He was sitting astride it and it started to hiss; so he left it and made his way home. No sooner had he got there when there was a loud explosion and half the beach rained down on his wee house. I think he was lucky.

The battle of the Atlantic was in full swing, ships were being sunk galore and many's a dead seaman was washed up as well. The Irish army from Dunree fort or Leenan would arrive and take the corpse away in what seemed to be an old packing crate unlike the lovely varnished coffins with all the trimmings you were used to seeing. It was so cold and stark to see a person half rotted and eaten away by the salt water, seagulls and fishes. I saw several like that and at that age it is something you don't forget easily. They were of all nationalities but mostly British and there was a gruesome way of spotting the bodies – we looked for flocks of seagulls a bit off shore. You had to wait for the tide to wash the body in and keep throwing stones at the bloody seagulls. It must have been a hard time on sailors, God bless them. I remember seeing a hatch cover from the *Empress of Britain* floating in and a few years later meeting up with a deck steward on the *Queen Mary* who had been on the *Empress* when she was sunk off Malin Head. So it is really a small world too. He told me all about the battle and of the acts of bravery he witnessed that day both during the battle and after when they were in the sea covered with burning oil. By the way, the *Empress of Britain* was a luxury passenger ship from the Empress line. All their ships were called *Empress* of something or other, and they sailed all over the world.

Going to Mass on a Sunday was a big affair. We had two choices – either walking almost five miles to Clonmany and get home about 2 pm or cross over in the boat to Lagg and get home about the same time; so guess which one we took. The boat was about twenty feet long and I have a photograph of it with thirty people sitting and standing. It had four oars with, I think, two men to each oar and a couple of basins to bale out the water as it came in through the cracks. There were two crossing points and both boats looked the same but I loved crossing in Corr Cooper's boat as it was more scary because of the narrows and the 'captain' had to give out more orders. Any slacking at all and the boat would have been caught in the breakers and capsized. I think a big lot was left to providence; maybe too much, for when I grew older and travelled a bit, on my return I shuddered to think on the chances that were taken every Sunday in the name of religion.

It was a lovely time to be young, for the simplicity of the people was great. I remember one day the boat couldn't cross because the tide was running too rough and Lizzy McLaughlin had been planning to go 'forrard' to receive holy communion. So she said to my mother, 'Well, Sarah, I'll just go home and eat a holy picturr.' My brother Terry exaggerated a wee bit, for on telling the story, he made out it was a picture off the wall, glass, frame and all, but I'll leave that to yourselves; it wasn't just like that. I think it was a wee one out of her prayer book; still that's faith for you. It's the kind we sing about at the retreats. 'Faith Of Our Fathers' and all that.

It was from that wee boat that we watched the ship getting blitzed while the two neutral Irish planes flew past and did nothing. I wonder to this day if the Irish pilots remember that encounter.

The wee chapel was only opened on Sundays for Mass and after the Mass we had Benediction and Devotions which made the whole service very long indeed. It was opened on request through the week for funerals. Swallows would nest in it, gaining access through the odd broken window. During Mass they would fly in and out of any openings and it added a wee bit of interest to the proceedings.

Speaking of funerals, I remember seeing one coming to that wee chapel and as the slope of the hill was too steep the coffin was slung low almost touching the ground. Walking about fifty yards in front of it were a number of women, about ten of them, in their bare feet and wrapped in shawls, keening as was the custom of the day. I can see it yet as if it were yesterday like a picture out of the penal days.

It was common to see people with their shoes or boots tied around their necks going to Mass on Sunday and putting them on at the chapel door. So naturally I imitated them and do you know that after the holiday was over and when I got back to Derry my shoes were always too small? Oh and by the way, the kitchen too appeared to have shrunk because we had gotten so used to the wide open spaces. It took us a day or two to acclimatise ourselves again to the confines of our wee house in Fountain Hill. My family, when we meet, always talk about the Isle and we relive a lot of happy times alas gone for ever, for the people we grew up with are either dead or have emigrated, and the younger generation would only be embarrassed if we started telling some of the antics or the way life was sixty years ago.

I talked of the harvesting which was before machinery had reached Donegal, for I was twelve or thirteen before a horse-drawn reaper was introduced in the Isle and half the population turned out to see it in Willy Billy's field, next to the Slate House. It was a wonder to behold, all right, for till then all the reaping was done by hand and scythe.

Before I really leave the Isle let me give you a small example of some of the names. Although Peter Oggy was young Peter, he was a brave age when he died, and there was John Johnny Wullie, Peter Sheila, John Wullie, the Owny Briens, Dan John Wullie, Susie Peter and so on, the John Dinnys, Lizzy at the Shore, Lizzy Jim, Wullie at the Shore, Mary in Cuill, Betty at the Lough. I could go on with more and it saddens me to think that all these people are gone now and the old way of naming them is dying out too. I never bothered to ask for a surname at the time, for it was unnecessary with their Christian names like such, but now when I read of a death from the Isle in the paper I wish they would put in the proper name that all their friends knew instead of Willie Doherty or Elizabeth McDaid. How about John Wullie or Lizzy Jim? Then at least I would know who the deceased was.

MEN OF THE HOUSE
– AND WOMEN

My brother Gerard and his cousin Connie fell in with a couple of high-flyers and started to smuggle in a big way. It was thrilling at night listening to them talking over the narrow escapes they had with the Water-Rats, as the Customs officers were known. I would wait up for them coming home after an overnight run and make them up a big fry of bacon, eggs, sausages and black pudding, and they would give me a couple of £100 notes to run up to Selfridge's fish-and-chip shop to change for them. They had the use of a suite of rooms in the Gresham Hotel in Dublin paid by the syndicate and all they had to do was drive a loaded lorry from point A in the North here to point B in the South. Usually Derry to Dublin. I would like to say here that it was strictly foodstuffs and not drugs or such, as this sort of thing hadn't reared its ugly head yet. They loved the excitement plus the added bonus of putting one over on the authorities who wouldn't allow them to work in the first place.

It was great and I delighted in it too, for I remember one night they were chased by His Majesty's customs and their orders were, if it looked like they were going to get caught, to leave the trucks and clear off. Well, the chase was on and in those days the customs used Ford Pilot cars with V8 engines and they were superior to any other. Realising that they hadn't a chance, Connie and Gerard hopped out of the trucks and ran over the fields taking the keys with them. The trucks were confiscated and towed to the customs lock-up at Goraghwood to be processed next day but during the night the two boyos broke into the lock-up and drove their trucks out again and on to Dublin. My mother was never off her knees, God love her, for she always worried about Gerard but sure while his was a short life he enjoyed it to the full.

When the light went out on Gerard nine years after my father's death, my mother's light started to dim too, for it seemed her whole world was being taken away from her. Gerard was a great character all together and he was the apple of her eye, always full of mischief; it was a crime that he was left with all that responsibility so young. He was only seventeen or so when my father died. He enjoyed going to country dances and such, and there wasn't a hint of sophistication about him and his friends were with him to the end, for after he had taken care of the family he had a light-hearted attitude to life. In the last six months of his life while working in England he contracted some illness that completely paralysed him and he dropped from a normal twelve stone to about five. His pals young and old came in to see him and wept openly but he joked all the time with them and when they were leaving he asked Mannix to stay behind and he spent a long time talking with him. He then sent for all the family and shook hands with us all, kissed my mother goodbye and closed his eyes. I wish you could have known him.

Mannix was a year younger but they had been very close and it seems that when they were younger they looked so alike that even my mother had to think twice sometimes when addressing them. When Gerard was smuggling, a detective tried to call his bluff one day, saying he saw him in such a place and Gerard produced Mannix and really confused him.

Our house had a groundfloor front room and back kitchen, with a long hall that ran from the street to the backyard, and next floor up were two bedrooms with two attic bedrooms above that. The attic bedrooms' ceilings sloped with the roof and each had a skylight on the slates and when we as children were put to bed at night and my mother thought she had the front room to herself, the calling would start: 'Ma, can I have a drink of water? Ma, can I have . . .' and so it went on.

One night everything was too quiet, so she went to the foot of the stairs to listen to the silence, when in through the door from the street burst Gerard completely out of breath, followed by Mannix. He too was breathless after running a race. The course was a semi-obstacle one which started for one runner at the top of Fountain Hill on Spencer Road and for the other at the bottom of Fountain Hill on Duke Street. The idea was that one would run up Duke Street, the other down Spencer Road towards each other to meet at Cafolla's ice-cream parlour, do one turn round the revolving doors and head for home, dressed in their birthday suits. As this had been going on for a while, they were always assured of an audience. I guess they must have been the original streakers. They were about seven years old at the time.

Well the mantle of 'man of the house' went to Mannix and this he wore till his death too. I often wonder if Gerard asked Mannix to stay with the family, for he never married although he could have; but he never disclosed what he and Gerard talked about that last time. Mannix was another great character, a fact borne out at his funeral by the numbers that turned out, and I was astonished at the number of young lads less than half his age who attended the Mass. He was very quick to see, initiate or take part in a joke or wag on his old mates. He also worried about and visited old pals who had seen healthier days. He was all right. The night in 1972 when the Top of the Hill bar was hit by two gunmen, five people were shot dead, Mannix had just got up from his chair, gone in to the toilet, heard the commotion, run out to find all the dead and dying on the floor, and his chair cut to ribbons with bullets. He always thanked God for the kidneys He gave him, for on another occasion he stepped out of the bookies to the toilet next door, heard a rumble, and stepped out again to find the bookies blown away with an IRA bomb. Thank God there were no casualties. There was a warning given but Mannix had not been in a position to hear it.

Before I leave Mannix for a while let me tell you a wee bit of his philosophy. He didn't want more out of life than a pick and shovel. His motto was: 'Nobody is going to take it off you!' He always said, 'You never hear anybody praise a good job nor anybody run down a bad job.' You can work that out for yourselves. He just needed enough to get by. He died at sixty-eight or so and all through his working life he always handed in his wages unbroken. Mind you, he got taken care of during the week: there was always the price of a pint or a bet. He was 'old-date' in his ways, too, and at times thought I was a bit brash but we got on great. It's at times like now that he would be of great help to me writing this, for he was an avid reader and took a great interest in local history present and past. He was interested in people without being nosy. I think he looked at me with disgust sometimes if I couldn't remember who he was talking about, forgetting that there was almost a ten-year gap in our ages.

Terry, the youngest of that set, died at sixty-eight too. Those steps at the top of our hill were nearly Terry's headstone, for a horse and four-wheeled cart, loaded with beer and whiskey, ran away at the top of the hill, got out of control, came out over the steps and fell on top of him. The track of the horseshoe was in Terry's head until he died. He was seven years old at the time. Many years later he gave a man a lift along the road who turned out to be a retired policeman and as is the wont of the police he started to ask Terry where he came from and further questions like that. When Terry told him, he said he would never forget his first accident call-out and described it in detail, finishing up saying, 'The little boy was dead.' Terry did the wee bit out of the Bible, for he got the man to put his hand in the wound . . .

Terry was born with a lucky-cap – that is a cap of membrane on the baby's head at birth – and during his life he was extremely lucky, which manifested itself at Christmastimes, birthdays, First Communions and Confirmations, for he always 'shot a rise' in the bookies and he would come in to his wife and throw a fistful of notes on the table and say, 'Rig the weans out, Maggy!' It always came at the right time for her. They have fourteen children all alive, with most of them married, so you can imagine that house when they all gather on family occasions. The caul was a sought-after treasure amongst seamen, who regarded it as a safeguard against drowning, and it would be carried about usually in a tin box. I have seen an uncle of mine with one.

Terry in his teens was a bit of a glamour boy, with natural blond wavy hair which was the whole go then. When he was walking out with Maggy, he would take over the kitchen every night and give himself a bath; there were no bathrooms in those days, only a big zinc bath that was carried in and out as it was needed. One night in particular he had the usual bath, got dressed and with the hair gleaming was just about ready to step out, when for some reason or other he decided to poke up the fire. To help it along he poured some paraffin oil on it. Now it was a Stanley range and it took a while to light up, so Terry lifts off one of the lids to see what was happening and it gave a whoof and ignited. Terry put the lid back on again and, without checking in the mirror, went on over the town to pick up Maggy. Nobody had the heart to tell him that he was like Al Jolson in blackface. The soot had puffed up round him and left him all black but since it was during the blackout nobody would have noticed until he came in to the light. I wasn't there so I can't tell you the reaction but I'm sure it was hilarious.

Terry liked his locks so much that he answered an ad in one of the papers for hair oil. There were seven bottles marked for each day in the week and I can tell you Gerard had a field day here, for Terry hid the bottles in old coat pockets up in the attic lobby and Gerard would change the days just to see what would happen. It was a scream but my mother was a bundle of nerves in case Terry would cop on.

Terry and Maggy married, I think, in 1945 near the end of the war and Mary Lou was born the following year and you would have thought the wean was Gerard's by the fuss he made of it. Sad to say he didn't have long, for he died at the end of that year. Terry and Maggy took over the empty shop in Duke Street just to have the living quarters above and while they were there the Yanks started to move out of their camp at Springtown and this is when I first heard the word 'squatting' used. I always thought it meant 'to sit', but a different meaning or interpretation was given to it at this time. Anyway what it boiled down to was, the Yanks moved out of their Nissen-hut camp, and the gerrymandered, overcrowded, homeless Derry nationalists moved in.

There was good reason for doing this, for the Unionist-controlled Londonderry Corporation had the Catholic population by the throat and at this stage were not building houses for nationalists (or come to think of it for loyalists either). It was often the case that one or two of a family would get married and would move into their parents' home; thus two or three families were reared in the one house. It is hard for those who haven't experienced this state of affairs to imagine what it was like but it was a nightmare for those who had to suffer it. I mention this about the housing, for as soon as Gerard got to hear about the Yanks moving out, he made a beeline out to the camp and commandeered the hut that had been used as the chapel for Terry, Maggy and Mary Lou. Lucky that my mother in her wisdom talked them out of moving, for it wasn't too long after that the corporation started to build houses in the Creggan for the Catholics and in Irish Street in the Waterside for Protestants; so Terry got a house in Creggan.

Incidentally the corporation cut the rod to beat themselves with here, for a couple of decades later it all backfired. To go back to the poor squatters in the camp, they were stuck there for twenty-five to thirty years. The first thing the corporation did was to cut off all services but after some argument and discussion I think they were partly restored. Through time the huts deteriorated but the officials refused to accept responsibility and the poor people lived no better than itinerants on the move. Springtown camp became a village on its own and a couple of generations were born there. It is one of the many black marks on the record of Londonderry Corporation and I wonder if there is any regret about it at all. I doubt it. Terry and Maggy moved to the Creggan, to 10 Dunree Gardens to be exact, and reared their large family. Lucky enough, he got a move to the Waterside just at the outbreak of the Troubles, for the Waterside was relatively quiet at that time.

Terry and Maggy got on with their lives and he opened a newsagent's, with fresh fruit and vegetables, sweets and sundries, which is still run by one of the sons. Maggy was a very retiring girl. She always seemed very quiet and only spoke when spoken to and it would seem Terry had all the get-up-and-go for the two of them. Terry and me always got on like a house on fire although he denied me publicly in the paper because I stood for the Social Democratic and Labour Party in a council by-election – with him having the wee shop he didn't want to lose custom, so he placed a notice in the paper disowning me. It was laughable at the time and I said he was like Saint Peter denying Christ. We didn't fall out as was expected but I used to look at him every now and again and say with a deep voice, 'Terry, you denied your own brother . . .' I know he was sorry it happened, but sure if it hadn't, I couldn't tell you about it now. There was always a soft spot for Terry with my mother, aye and with all the family, because of his sterling work with my father. He did not know this but it was there all the same.

I had five sisters and I suppose you could say I was spoiled; they wouldn't let the wind of the fire blow on me and sometimes that annoyed me. Moira worked in the Star shirt factory as a patent turner and with the war in full swing the factories were going flat out. She brought work home at night and my sister Pauline and I would do it. It was easy when you were shown how but I guess that's all done by machinery now. Moira had a couple of pals, Eileen Bryson – she was all into movies and Hollywood – and Briege Starrett, a workmate in the Star. The young women and men in those days would have 'walked the

Strand': that is to say, in the evenings after work they would walk for leisure the length of the Strand Road (about a mile) and it was there that many a romance blossomed. It was known as the Strand Road parade and rightly so. It may seem tame but it was there that you set your sights on your prospective partner for life. A younger group, early teens to twenty, took over Carlisle Road and paraded up and down for a couple of hours at night from 8 o'clock till 10.30 meeting the same boys and girls and eyeing each other up. Many a future marriage was sparked off there too. Incidentally there wasn't a policeman in sight as there was no need for them.

The flicks were over about 10.45 and most families were in by 11 o'clock. And so it was with Moira, Philomena, Sheila, Roisin and Pauline. It wasn't an easy job rearing five young girls during the war years, for we had all the allied forces of the world passing through our wee town; my mother, like many other mothers, had her work cut out for her. Philomena, as I said earlier, was apprenticed to a dressmaker. Philomena and Sheila were more an age, so for a while they went to *céilí* dances together. There was a great nationalist spirit at that time and as the Crown forces or their allies were not admitted, my mother knew my sisters were safe enough at these dances. It was at one of these *céilí*s that Philomena met her man Johnny Carlin. After the usual courtship they married and came to live in our house until they got a flat in Iniscarn Road in the Creggan. They then transferred to a house in Eastway Gardens, just a street away, where they raised six girls and two boys; during the hostilities in the early seventies they left the Creggan to live in the Waterside. Johnny died in 1993 and though all the girls are married they live in the town close by, so Philla has plenty of company.

Sheila too worked in a shirt factory. She had pals from the factory and, as I said, the usual recreations were the pictures, *céilí*s or walks. Sad to say there were few drama schools in her growing-up days, for she loved acting, and at the drop of a hat she would recite Robert Emmet's speech from the dock. Starting off with her arms folded, she would declaim, 'I have but a few more words to say – I'm going to my cold and silent grave . . .' and whoever was caught was relieved when she came to the last sentences: 'Then, and not till then, let my epitaph be written. I have done.' She had the cheek to take a bow after this.

Roisin and Pauline had similar careers. Roisin, like Moira and Sheila, had flaming red hair and she too worked in a shirt factory. Listening to some of her escapades with older girls in the factory, I realise she must have been a handful, full of mischief. It's strange that Moira, Sheila and Roisin never married, for it seemed that they had plenty of suitors. Pauline met and married Eugene McCormick from Ardmore and he really did become one of the family and, thank God, still is. They have six sons and one daughter named Sarah after my mother. Eugene was a taxi driver when he met Pauline and his stories about his taxiing days are hilarious. I call in to see them most mornings when leaving Siobhán, my daughter, to work and I always come away laughing. He has a different story every day but I liked the one about his feeding the chickens. His boss Charlie Bradley kept free-range chickens on a wee farm a couple of miles out of town and every day they would take up their feed which consisted of boiled spuds mixed with meal. Rather than go into the mucky hen-run, they would stand outside the high chainlink fence and roll the feed into balls and pitch them over. The poor ould hens would run around after the balls of food but more often than not they got hit over the head and were knocked out. This is what I call 'getting your grub threw at you'.

They kept a couple of pigs too and one day Charlie asked Eugene to go to the railway station and pick up a fare and at the same time take a sow pig up to the wee farm. Eugene looks at the clock and says to himself, 'I'd better go to the station first or this fare will get some other taxi.' So away he sails with the pig in the front seat and picks up a very nice lady, a wee bit snooty, mind you, for she made comment about the pig in the front. Sure you would never get away with that nowadays. This is a sample of his stories. The Troubles weren't easy on Pauline and Eugene but that's their own story. Thank God they survived. That is a short history of the family I was blessed with and through all the trials and tribulations of growing up we were always very close. To this day I always class the home of Moira, Sheila and Roisin as the 'house', even though they have moved from the place where I was born to Gobnascale at the top of the hill.

BUTTERMILK, SHOES,
ARMY BOOTS

There was very little traffic in those days, as nearly everything was transported by horse and cart. Buttermilk came on the
back of horse-drawn two-wheeled carts. The buttermilk man
stopped at certain places and he measured off a pint or quart
into your jug or tin can with the measures that hung by the
churn. There was no talk of hygiene but, come to think of it,
I never heard of anyone dying of buttermilk poison. The buttermilk actually had pieces of butter still floating on it as if to

prove its authenticity and that's why scone bread tasted so different to the stuff nowadays. Now, the sweet milk was delivered daily by horse and cart, fitted to hold six 30-gallon cans and here again the usual pint and quart measures were used. Bottled milk was mainly for the swankier customer, and after a while a wax carton was introduced but that cost more, so it wasn't a great success. My mother didn't go for that at all, probably because it was dearer, but she always said it didn't taste right.

We had two deliveries, one by a man called Eddie Hamilton with a horse and cart and six big cans of milk, and the other was a girl called Noeleen McCandless who carried two 2-gallon cans from door to door and measured the milk out on the step. Her aunt kept cows in the backyard of an end-terraced house where she lived in Violet Street and after milking the cows in the morning, she, along with her niece, walked round the district delivering the milk and it still warm. The aunt then walked the cows a mile or so outside the town to graze and in the evening this performance was repeated. Looking back, it seems to me a hard way to earn a crust. Someone has painted a mural of her taking her cows out or bringing them back – sure it doesn't matter which, she looks tired anyway.

One day I was being chased for some mischief I'd done on Gerard and was running like the clappers up Duke Street. I noticed a buttermilk cart outside Davy Kennedy's pub, so as Gerard was gaining fast on me – or as we say, 'taken up on me', I nipped out sharp and turned on the buttermilk tap and ran on. Gerard, good citizen, ran over to turn it off, when out of the pub stepped, guess who? – the owner. Well there was hell to pay – but I got away. Once, many years later, after I had started going to sea and was home on leave, I had occasion to work one night in the same bar as relief for the barman John Nicell who played football for a local amateur team. The pubs in those days, unlike now, were a man's domain, as no lady would have crossed the door. Sad to say it's all changed now (that's my own opinion!) but anyway this old fellow with a big walrus moustache came in. The bar was nice and quiet, so the old guy got talking to me. I was mesmerised looking at the Guinness froth on his moustache and he seemed an ould blether, like myself, I suppose. When he heard I did a bit of boxing he started on about his younger brother, how good a boxer he was, and that the last he heard of him was in 'Signapore', as he called it. You know, you have to have the patience of Job to be a barman and I had to listen to the exploits of his brother and, worst of all, agree with everything he said. Well, about two months later I was sailing through the Pacific making a call at Fiji, and who should come aboard to pay his respects to the captain and represent His Majesty the King but the 'bould' younger brother! The ould fellow was speaking the truth after all, for the younger brother was the highest ranking government wheeler-dealer out there in a radius of 700 miles. I know it must have seemed forward of me because of his very high rank but I took the chance when I heard him speak and made myself known to him. He was taken aback when I pinpointed the exact district he came from and informed him of his brother's health, and he would have stood all day talking, only duty called him to meet the captain and other dignitaries. I was only a waiter but I knew more about the guy than they did and he seemed a civil fellow. He was Oxford educated and that was no mean thing at the time. I'm talking now of 1950, when I met him.

I recall an open day in Ebrington Barracks before the war and I'm sure it must have had something to do with Edward VIII's taking the throne while the Empire and all the loyal subjects rejoiced. The barracks was thrown open to the public and there was a lot of drilling and showing off, cannons and tables of food, the like I never saw before. It would have made you get excited maybe and join up even. Needless to say it was all in vain as far as I was concerned anyway, for I was only eight years old and to crown it out yer man let them down, he abdicated. Sadly all this grandeur stopped at the outbreak of war and the South Wales Borders were moved out to make room for the Yanks. I missed the soldiers out swaggering with their canes, boots shining and puttees wrapped round the trouser bottoms – a hand over from the Indians. They were an orderly lot, rarely in trouble, just a peacetime army and quite a few married local girls, so when it came time for them to move there was a lot of weeping and gnashing of teeth as the wives and sweethearts were left behind.

My schooldays, as you can probably guess from this account, weren't great. Instead of going to the local school with the rest of my friends, my mother sent me to the Christian Brothers and as I said, there was very little Christianity about them: they beat the daylights out of me. In those days you never complained because 'you must have been up to something' and the teacher was always right. Not so, as I know, and I still have the mental scars to remind me: getting lifted out of your seat by your sidelocks or having a big bull-clip hung on the point of your nose. School for me was a nightmare. I won a scholarship to the Municipal Technical College and stayed there for eighteen months. All the scholarship exams were geared towards the civil service or the forces, engineers, gunners and such. Well, there was no way I was going to England to train and possibly finish up with a cap badge with a crown above my head. Enough of Irish blood had been spent for England and I was making sure mine wasn't going to mix with it. I found a job as a shoe salesman, it got me out of school and I was happy.

The firm I worked for had three branch shops, so, when they hadn't the shoe in one shop, I would have been called to take the shoes to wherever. It was great, this, and the shops were within walking distance of each other, so it broke the monotony to get out, to see what was going on in the outside world. The manager of my branch, John Bradley, was ancient, probably about twenty-seven and there wasn't a lot of conversation. It was also better than fitting some old farmer whose boots were sometimes still 'leggard' with cow manure. John Bradley – still alive at time of writing – was cute enough to leave that kind of customer to me. The firm also had a boot-and-shoe repair place, and after six months I got a transfer there. My mother was elated. I was in my fifteenth year then.

That period was very happy, for I was in with three others known as journeymen; I was a first-year apprentice. There was also a second-year apprentice called Jim Nicell, and he and I struck it off together. The crack was good for Jim and myself re-enacted all the movies of the day, and our shoot-outs and death scenes were real Hollywood classics. Cecil B, eat your heart out! All this would take place during working hours, and the old journeymen – they were in their forties – thought we were crazy. If only things could be as simple nowadays.

Big Johnny McKeown, my boss, stood about six feet six inches to my five feet four inches, so can you imagine me wearing his raincoat. Well I did, for it was raining one day and as I was about to go home for my lunch Big Johnny says: 'Ginger, take my coat; it'll keep you dry.' God bless us! it would have kept half of Derry dry, it was that big, and greasy to boot. I walked over the bridge looking like Dopey the dwarf in *Snow White*, with the greasy coat trailing the ground and the sleeves six inches too long. To crown it out, the factory girls were just getting out for lunch and whilst I hadn't yet started going out with Agnes my wife there was a good chance I would see her and she me. That's the way romance blossomed in those days. I made sure always to bring my coat in future. I was sixteen and the war was just over.

Before I leave the war I must mention my cousin Sonny –
I never did get his Christian name; I'm sure it wasn't Sonny
– but anyway he called in to our house with his rifle and full
marching kit, straight from the front. While having his tea in
our wee kitchen – it was like an oven – he kept his great coat
on all the time, sat up close to the range which was red hot and
started to shiver and shake. My mother, his aunt, thought he
had the cold, and told him to see the doctor but she mightn't
have bothered for the poor lad had malaria and died a very short
time after. I never saw him after that day. He fought in Malaya
and Burma but on the way home via the Suez Canal and the
Mediterranean his outfit was thrown into Sicily for the invasion
of Italy.

When I started in McKeown's my wages were a penny
ha'penny an hour, and when I left it had risen to sevenpence
ha'penny. This was in old money, of course; today it would be
less than £1.50 a week. Still, I don't think I should complain
too much, for you only get out of anything what you put in.
One person I will always remember was Charlie Brown. He was
the general runabout for the boss (there's one in every firm) and
he would make up the wages and give you your time on a wee
slip of paper. We worked an eight-hour day and since naturally
I was normally five or ten minutes late in the morning, I had
this deducted from my wages at the end of the week. My time
slip read something like this:

Mon	7hr 53m
Tues	7hr 56m
Wed	7hr 51m
Thur	7hr 54m
Fri	7hr 52m
Sat	3hr 56m
Total	43hr 22m

So I was thirty-eight minutes short and at one and a half pence an hour this was deducted from my wages. Now this was before the age of computers but Charlie worked it out anyway. Needless to say Big Johnny died and the two nephews got left the business and gave Charlie the 'business', so it all comes round to you one way or another.

I started to box in the ring and got a few fights under my belt. I am sad to say a lot of my opponents have since died – but of course that was years later. Training became like a religion to me and I attained a very high degree of fitness, in other words I became very fit indeed. I trained every night in the gym and ran about six miles in the morning dressed in two pairs of trousers and a couple of sweaters and the heaviest of hobnail boots, just like the old-time fighters. The idea of the heavy boots was when you got into the ring with the lighter boxing boots on you were supposed to feel like a ballet dancer. It sounds like a brag but it is just a statement of fact that my first thirteen fights all finished in the first round and I got to the point where I thought all I had to do was touch you and you would fall. Then I ran up against a wily old campaigner called Jim Murray. I couldn't get near him and he stole the fight by just staying out of my way. Jim has since died but losing that fight to him taught me a good lesson – that I needed a wee bit more than a good right hand. I took more of an interest in what old Jimmy 'Spider' Kelly was doing in the ring but it was about then that I got the call, just like in the Bible, to come to the defence of my country, Éire, in her time of need.

The state of emergency was not yet over or at least nobody told me, so, as in the the song, I was off to Dublin in the green, in the green. I landed outside Portobello Barracks and joined up. I lied about my age, saying I was eighteen, so I was provisionally accepted. That night I was moved out to the Curragh Camp but I already knew I made a mistake in leaving home and

I cried myself to sleep. In the army they don't waste much time, for the bugle blew or called, or whatever a bugle does, at 6 o'clock the next morning and I really wasn't used to the roaring and shouting from the corporal, who incidentally had a whopper of a lisp. Between 'up and at it' and 'out lights', he was great. I figured at this stage that I'd made my bed, so I may as well lie in it but I'll never forget that first morning out in the square when the twenty of us – how could there be nineteen or twenty more guys like me in the world to get into a fix like this! – got our eyes opened to army life. It was like Barnum's circus.

We were a closely knit fighting unit going to defend Ireland from her enemies from whatever side and when we got our rifles and web (army talk for your bullet and bayonet belt) I couldn't get back to the billet quick enough to shoot my roommates as they came through the door. Thank God I didn't get bullets with it. I can still remember the name and date of my rifle: Lee Enfield, 1912. Maybe it was one of the rifles from the *Asgard*. It doesn't matter now, for I broke it the first day I got it and I often wonder how many fellows it shot by accident after I gave it back. The safety catch sheared off. so it was always in a firing position. Well, it's too late now to be crying over spilt milk.

My platoon paraded next to the Irish-speaking battalion and I may as well have been in Basutoland, for sad to say the Irish language was foreign to me. At school Irish was taught one hour a week and it wasn't taught but battered into you or out of you depending which way you looked at it. On church parade I never heard as much swearing and cursing in all my life. The wee old sergeant, or should I say, the old wee sergeant? – he was no bigger than me but twice as broad and I think he was a handover from Mickey Collins's time when height didn't count – would come up and stand in front of you and call you bad names. Then we would all go off to Mass, marching to the tune of 'My Mary Of The Curling Hair'. I waltzed to that later when I was out in civvy street.

One thing that stands out from that time was the open-air eating arrangement we had. Since it was such good weather, our mess was outside in the square. It was a scramble between you and the birds swooping and snatching the food off the table.

There isn't a lot to be said about my army career save to say I was glad when they told me to go home and come back when I was eighteen. It seems the Derry police must have been asked for a character reference and then my cover was blown, for according to them I was under age. At this time I was in about three weeks and shaping up, when one morning out – I don't know why it's not 'in' – the square, the sergeant called my name and number and asked me to take one pace forward, which I did, thinking it was promotion, maybe general or at least major-general, whichever was the best, but no such luck. On hindsight I was luckier, for he looked me up and down disdainfully and said, 'Take your web and equipment back to the quartermaster's stores.' He added a PS which I never forgive him for to this day: 'A waste of a good uniform.' Pity I didn't ask him to hold on to it till I came back, eh? for he would be still holding it.

That wasn't the end, for I guess they figured money had been spent on me to bring me to the peak of fitness which I now enjoyed, so they were going to make sure I would work it off. The next stop was the Bog of Allen to work turf. It didn't bother me at all, for it took me back to my Isle of Doagh days, where we worked at turf in the hill. Along with a gang of others I was trucked out at 8 am and back at 4.30 pm, with no parades or dressing up, wearing no uniforms but just fatigues. I was finally discharged after thirty-five days, the reason given on my discharge book: 'Not having been finally approved'. So at age sixteen and a half I was an ex-soldier. It looked like Ireland would have to fight her own battles.

THE SQUARE RING

After being drummed out of the army I came home to Derry, got my old job back in McKeown's and resumed my boxing activities. I boxed regularly both in Derry and Belfast. My trainer-manager was Dan Doherty who signed me up to a ten-year contract but really I was only playing at it, for while the fights were real enough and, I might say, hard enough, I wasn't getting paid enough. The Ulster Hall in Belfast had twice-weekly bills and I seemed to be a favourite there, for in one year alone I boxed thirty-three times, so they must have liked me. The money wasn't great but it was the going rate: if I won I got £2.10s and if I lost £1.10s. Into the bargain, if I didn't turn up for the fight there were at least six boxers, every bit as good as me, to jump in at a minute's notice and take my place. Glad to say, I won most of my fights inside the distance, so it kept me from taking too much punishment and my features weren't disfigured too much. I boxed under the name of Red Doran because I had a mop of red hair but there were two other Derry Reds – Deehan and McCauley – and the funny thing about it was, we had similar lives. We all boxed at one time or another, worked in the catering trade, and, believe it or not, later I introduced them both to the sea. They are both dead now and whenever the subject of boxing in the town comes up the three Reds are mentioned.

Derry had more than its share of characters and somehow the boxing game attracted them. It was great to hear their comments both during and after the fight and you had to have extra thick skin or you would never strip off at all. I remember one night while watching a slow-moving fight – more of a waltzing competition – when some wag shouted, 'Put the lights out', and the unmistakable voice of 'Hawker' Lynch answered, 'Naw, don't! I'm reading the paper.' My days in the gym were very happy; we had great camaraderie. Some, but, sad to say, not enough of the old boxers are still around. A lot, as they say in boxing parlance, have taken the long count.

My idol and everybody else's at that time was Jimmy 'Spider' Kelly, ex-British and Empire featherweight champion. He got the name Spider because when you were fighting him it seemed he had as many arms as a spider and he hit you from all angles. He was making a comeback in 1946, for professional boxing had been suspended during the war, along with a lot of other big spectator events. There were mainly a couple of reasons for this suspension: one being that the talent was in the army and secondly it was deemed unwise to have large gatherings of people because of the air raids. Now that the war had ended Spider was matched with Stan Hawthorn, a southpaw from Newcastle upon Tyne. Kelly, being out of shape and grossly overweight, had to work to get down to near his fighting weight and fitness. It was very hard to do after a six-year lay-off, but with plenty of sparring and roadwork he made it. I learned more from sparring with Spider and watching his every move than with all the trainers or coaches put together. Like myself, he found it hard to pass on or convey his skills, so you watched and learned. Hawthorn was young and strong and youth triumphed in the end and Spider got beaten; so the band or parade passed him by. Sadly a fighter always thinks there is still one fight left in him; he is tempted by another pay night and it's then he gets abused and finishes up punch-drunk.

I boxed with Spider on a few bills after that but he was only a shadow of his former self and his purses were very low. It was indeed sad to see a dancing master like himself having to carry his own gear into a one-off boxing arena in some wee provincial town and box third-rate opponents for buttons. Some of them wouldn't have been good enough to lace his boots. Still that's the fight game and the hardest crown to carry is success; as long as you are winning you are a great fellow but drop a decision or two and you are a has-been. My motto, though, is: 'It's better to be a has-been than a never-will-be.'

Every boxing dressing-room has at least one ex-pug that has taken too many punches and Derry had its share. I can remember Johnny 'Cuttems' fighting Columba McNulty, posing as the 'Brown Bomber' and for this Columba was coated from head to foot with a brown stain. After the introduction in the centre of the ring the two boxers went back to their corners to come out fighting. Columba, sitting with his back to the corner, put his two hands on the ropes and his seconds tied them to the ropes so when the gong sounded he couldn't get out of his corner. Cuttems bate the head off him. Looking back, it was cruel but was considered funny at the time. I was certain I was not going to finish up like that.

Then there was Anthony McGowan, over the hill but still thinking there was a fight left in him. We young ones would use wee Anthony as a punchbag and the poor chap didn't know enough to say enough. I see him today and I feel ashamed of myself, for I ignorantly contributed to his state of health. Wee Anthony, as he was affectionately called, would accommodate us up-and-coming young bucks by sparring with us, and with the old trainer standing at the ringside calling instructions at you and yelling for you to do this and do that, hit him with this and hit him with that, the only one at the receiving end of all this was Anthony.

There was another wee hard nut called Nobby Lynch, ex-British Army and as regimental as I wasn't. I think he must have been one of the last of the old bare-knuckle fighters, for he seemed so old to us then. He had his hair cropped close and he shaved every day with his face shining and his boots to match. Although he was only five feet one inch he weighed about ten stone and not an ounce of surplus about him. To take him for a mug was a big mistake, and I saw it happen a few times with men a lot heavier than himself. He would dump them on the floor. I enjoyed many a spar with him.

I was part of the new crop coming up: heavyweights Barman Duffy and Mickey McMenamin, middleweights Joe Quinn, Leo Red Deehan and Tony Ward and a few old timers like Patsy Harkin, Anthony McGowan, Paddy Bonner, Ranger Harkin, Dan Canning and a 'rosary' of others, all from Derry. Bonner was very good in his day; it was just a pity he came up at the same time as Kelly or he might have done better.

I mentioned Joe Quinn there, for Joe and myself had great

respect for each other. Joe was a fully fledged middleweight, 11 stone 7 pounds to my 10 stone, but at sixteen years of age and fit, I was as strong as I was ever going to be. I delighted in sparring with Joe and these spars usually turned out to be as near the real thing as get out. I wouldn't give way to Joe nor he to me but I didn't realise the weight difference was significant until one night while I was fighting in Belfast and in the third round I was having bother focusing in on my opponent – I saw two of him – so I asked my seconds to throw in the towel. In the excitement I was thrown into the middle of the ring myself and, as that was not what I had intended, I turned to come back to my corner when the towel came sailing in from the other corner. I hope you can follow this so far. I learned two things from that night: firstly stay away from Joe Quinn and secondly that no matter how hard you think you are getting it the other guy is suffering too.

Now you might wonder how I was thrown into the centre of the ring. I'll try to explain. When the round is over and you come back panting out of breath to your corner, the second sits you down and pulls your legs out in front of you. He then proceeds to fill his mouth with water from the bottle that you thought was for you and sprays it all out over your face and body. Then he hits you with a wet sponge, talking to you all the while, giving you instructions: hit him with this, hook him with that, slip his left hand, cross over his lead, stay away from his right. During all this time the other second has his hand down the waistband of your trunks, pulling the waistband out to give you air, he says, but after a few fights I caught on to the reasoning of this. As soon as the gong sounds for the next round he has a fair grip on your pants in order to lift you practically out of your seat and deposit you in the centre of the ring. Oh, by the way, there would surely be a third second there to flap the towel and for what reason I never did understand, for all he was doing was moving cigarette smoke from the back of the hall to the ringside.

My manager, as I said, was Dan Doherty, although only in name, for he never took his entitlement of 10 per cent off me; but sure with the money I was getting it was hardly worth his while. One thing I do remember, I never knew who I was fighting most times until I would actually see him in the far corner of the ring. It was crazy, I know, but that was the way it was. I usually did well, so I guess my opponents were bigger palookas than I was. I think, too, that maybe I had a glass chin, for the two or three fights I lost were by knockout.

I didn't give any of my fights much thought, only that very often while sitting in my corner waiting for the referee to call me to the centre of the ring I used to ask myself, 'What on under God am I doing here? Sure I'd be better off at home!' and then the bell would sound and all that was forgotten. Boxing is a barbaric game and nobody can tell me different, for when the bell sounds you are going to try to knock another human being senseless. When the adrenalin is flowing and the fire is in the eye and your opponent is trying to hang in there, you seize on any weakness in his defence and batter him to pulp, for he is going to do the same to you, and as for the referee, he is no help, for he's only there to see you don't bite or scrape. When the bell sounds it is too late to cry for help because you are on your own. That square ring becomes the loneliest place in the world.

I should give a mention to our resident MC in Derry Guildhall, at that time our prime boxing arena. His name was Harry Doherty and he ran a small successful grocery, newsagent and sweet shop in the Creggan Estate. Harry really dressed for the fights, with the dress suit, bow tie, stiff front and cigar, and when he took the mike in the centre of the raised ring and started into a whole tirade, in a very cultured voice for the night, 'Ladies and Geenteelmen . . .' there was always an uproar of voices calling him 'Treacle Hole' and other such complimentary names. It was always good-natured banter and it added to the evening's entertainment and my boul' Harry always rose to the occasion: one night when someone called 'Treacle Hole' and Harry asked for order and got it, he announced over the mike, would the man who called that like to come up to the ring and face him? There was a wild scramble over seats as a couple of dozen men rushed the ring to get at Harry. Harry was tops and when they made him they broke the mould. He was never replaced.

Before I leave Harry I'd love to tell you a wee story about him. It goes something like this: one day a young woman traveller was in Harry's shop and this wee snottery-nosed boy about nine years old, with the torn jeans and greasy teeshirt and sneakers hanging together with bits of string, came in and interrupted Harry in conversation with your woman, saying, 'Two tookey buns.' Harry looked at your woman and then turned to the wee fellow said, 'No son, watch my lips', and he mouths out clearly, 'A cookie bun, please! Now go outside and come in again and ask for a cookie bun, please.' So the wee fellow goes out and comes back into the shop and goes over the same thing: 'Two tookey buns.' Harry, intent on impressing the girl and teaching the wee lad a bit of English, said again, 'Now go out and come in again and ask for two cookie buns, please. Now watch my lips. "Two cookie buns, please."' The wee fellow lifts his money, goes out, comes in again, throws the money down on the counter and says, 'Give me two tookey buns, you big tunt, you.' This is told around Derry as gospel, I thought I'd tell it too.

I took a dive twice in my boxing career, one in Larne and the other in Bombay. The dive in Larne came about because I was tired. You see, it was my third fight that week and when

I accepted it I was still warm, having just stepped out of the ring. I thought I was OK for the next night. I stayed overnight in Belfast and travelled out to Larne in the morning but I knew I had bitten off more than I could chew, for I was as stiff as a board. Still, I had accepted the fight and although people may say a lot about me, one thing they can't say is that I was piker. I turned up that night for the fight. After touching gloves in the first round I got on my bicycle and back-paddled just enough to keep out of harm's way but in the second round I figured I'd had enough, so I waited till my opponent slipped one over and it looked good, so I said to myself, 'Red, it's time to go home.' This is where the old dying scenes that Nicell and me enacted so often in McKeown's came into play. I crash-dived there and then. It was an open-air show in the town market and while I lay there being counted out, my thoughts went back to the great black heavyweight Jack Johnson.

I think it was Jess Willard he was boxing, and Johnson could have chewed him up and spat him out but he was between a rock and a hard place at the time. He had been acting the maggot round the world; what with running around with white women, taunting good fighters and then beating the hell out of them, he had very few friends. Above all this he was a good fighter but if he had beaten Willard that day in Texas, he would have been shot. He took the only way out and there's a great picture of him lying with his hand shielding the sun from his eyes, being counted out. Well that was what I was thinking of at the time I was being counted out in Larne but it is a long road . . . I boxed the same fellow, Billy Press, two weeks later and knocked him out in one.

Now, the other dive happened in Bombay in 1952 while I was working on the luxury liner RMS *Caronia*; but the story begins a year earlier. Our trainer on board was a Kiwi called Don Fowlks, a great chap altogether, and he arranged the fights through the ship's radio before we sailed from New York. I boxed in Auckland and gave exhibitions on deck but by the time I got to Colombo the fight season had closed. Bombay said they would accommodate us, so when we arrived there I was told to go to the main lounge. When I got up there, I could see all this 'brass' sitting around and I was hovering in the background waiting to catch the chief steward's eye to see what he wanted, when this ship's officer – I don't know who it was – said, 'Here he is now.' Naturally with all the brass there I looked around to see who they were talking about and it turned out to be me.

I was brought in to the middle of this bunch, everybody that was anybody was there from the skipper down. This awfully English chappy with a Sam Browne belt and a red sash round his shoulders stood up and I was introduced to him. He was Terry Adams, the chief of police left over from the Raj. India had left the Empire and fellows like him were left behind to smooth things out. He was quite a nice chappy but all this was way over my head and I was my usual bashful self so I never spoke a word. Adams enquired from the captain whether I would have time off and he committed himself, saying that as from now, I was off work till after the fight, which was to be against the Indian champion, Gene Raymond. Not bad considering the fight wasn't until Thursday and this was Saturday morning. On top of that, his batman was at my disposal. He came round in the morning or evening and took me sightseeing and my picture was in the papers while along the streets people were chatting me up and I lived up to it. I thought I was good and was not sure why I never got this treatment at home. (Lesson No. 1: there is nothing harder or heavier to carry than success; everybody was my friend and it was only a fight – and I had a lot of well-wishers.)

On the night of the fight I hadn't realised it was so big an occasion or meant so much and the dressing-room was packed with my shipmates. Then the music started, with the ship's band – part of Geraldo's – playing the 'Toreador's March' from *Carmen* as I made my way to the ring. It was then the realisation came to me of what it meant to the ship. First I was introduced to the Maharajah of Kashmir who had taken refuge in India whilst Pakistan and India fought over it. He was at the ringside and then I looked all around to see that the whole ringside was taken by the crew and passengers. It was a far cry from the Ulster Hall.

Lesson No. 2 had yet to come. I boxed this fellow's ears off and in the last round decided I could knock him out and it was here I came a cropper. I stumbled on a wee wrinkle in the canvas, fell onto a lovely right uppercut that he must have scraped the floor with before it connected with my chin and I went down. I knew what was happening. I heard the count 'eight, nine', got up, talked to myself, 'Just let me clinch with you and I'll be OK. If I get near you you'll never get rid of me. I'll tie you up and the bell will save me.' At this stage the fight was in the bag but the champ was too clever for me. He pushed me away from him, brought over another right cross and the lights went out.

Now the second lesson. The music had stopped, the crowd was quiet and when I came back to the empty dressing-room all the back-slappers had disappeared. I was there all alone to take the bandages off my hands and get dressed. I shuffled out of the stadium down the flight of steps to the street. It was about midnight and I was going to walk home to the ship when I heard the clip-clop of the horse and gharri coming down the street. I stopped and it stopped. The door opened and a voice said, 'Climb in, John', and it turned out to be our American chaplain, Father Martine. He said, 'I thought you would need someone to talk to', and we went home together and talked till the morning. He was a true friend. When you are a winner everybody wants to be your friend and I found out my real friends that night.

We sailed back a year later and Gene Raymond had retired, so my revenge was thwarted. The reigning champ was a younger lad about twenty-five. Come to think of it, he was three years older than me but he didn't have the experience of Gene Raymond. I got a message from a cab driver, saying the champ had to talk with me and me being the inquisitive type, I just had to see this guy to hear what he had to say. I met a man at the dock gate and he introduced himself as the champ's uncle, or so he said. We talked about my previous showing a year earlier against Gene Raymond. He thought, on that show-ing, I would be too good for him, so I was asked to take a dive. The money involved wasn't great; there was no 'big bucks' or anything like that but I was a sucker for a hard luck story and anyway I'd be leaving Bombay in another couple of days, so I agreed. I don't regret it. I had the same treatment as before, maybe a wee bit more subdued, seeing that I was getting used to it, but never the less some razzmatazz – and in the middle of the fourth round I dropped my hand. One came over, I think, from the balcony and it was 'Goodnight, Irene'.

We sailed from Bombay two days later and one of the crew, Colin Speery, approached me and, as he was a very good friend of mine, he put it to me straight. He said, 'You sold out.' Well what could I say? When he said, 'The boys lost a lot of money on you', I was speechless for I didn't realise that I was backed so heavily. I took it bad, for I was their hero. Needless to say, I went back the next year and was matched with the same fellow, same champ. I told the boys to put their lot on me and I came up with the goods, for I knocked him out in two rounds. The boys recouped in style; this I know, for they carried me out of the ring that night, a far cry from the first night I boxed there two years previously.

TOTALLY TROPICAL

By 1947, even though I enjoyed the boxing, I was still working in McKeown's and it seemed I was getting nowhere; so I decided I would like to go to England like the 'big boys' and as usual I got my wish. I went to Lancaster to distant cousins of my mother's and there checked in to the unemployment office, where I was given a job card to take out to a building site at the edge of town. As I had never been on a building site before I was disgusted with the muckiness of the place. I thought: typical Paddy – that's all he is good for! Out I went, still not quite eighteen, tiptoeing and choosing my steps – with all the other Paddies looking at me with amusement. When I arrived at the site hut and blushingly gave the girl my card, I was jolted into the real world with this unmerciful clatter and banging that shook the hut. In barged half a dozen Derrymen – they all knew me from boxing – demanding their wages to be made up right away if not sooner. They took my card out of the girl's hand and proceeded to tear it up saying to me, 'You're not starting here! Come with us.'

God, I thought, they're rough, but I followed them off the job and went back to my digs (declining the offer of joining them in theirs), which was a three-storey house with six or seven bedrooms and every inch of space let off. There must have been a million people in it and there were different grades of accommodation. For instance, beds cost more than stools or sofas, there was a pricelist for different types of chairs and if you were short of cash you could sleep in the kitchen with all the cooking going on around you. It was a proper madhouse and the address is still in my memory after all those years. It was 49 Leonard Gate, and was run by people called Rodgers, from Nelson Street, Derry. The story was that the Rodgers came into possession of the house when the old owner went senile and one of them got him certified.

An old fellow in the digs advised me to steer clear and go out to a local holiday camp; so away I goes, and lo and behold! I was taken on as a dishwasher, doubling at night as a redcoat. This was my introduction to the catering trade, at which I would labour for most of my working life. My time in the holiday camp passed so quickly that I don't have many memories of it except that I wrote to Mannix in Huddersfield and he came down to keep me company; I was still the wean. It wasn't his scene and when I left to come home a couple of weeks later he went up to Huddersfield again. After the last dance at night

I enjoyed grabbing Mannix and lining up in front of the stage like the Goldwyn Girls kicking up our legs and singing, 'Good night, campers'. Mannix was very embarrassed at it all but I really enjoyed it. It was the nearest I ever got to show business but it was for quite a short time, four or five weeks, and I left and came home to Derry.

The housing situation in Derry at this time was critical. There were no houses built at all since time began or it seemed that way. It was the accepted thing that when a daughter or son married they moved in with the parents or in-laws. In a wee two-bedroom house as many as two or three families would be reared at the same time and people had to take drastic measures to get a place to live. John Doherty, a boxing fan of mine, took over a small bar in town just to get a place to live. Since he was an architect he had no interest in running the bar, so he asked me to try my hand and I did. But the hours were long, so I decided to go for something better and I got in touch with Tommy Hasson, one of my cousins, who was a bedroom steward on the *Queen Elizabeth*. The wanderlust had gotten to me and I became one of the men that can't fit in. I think it was Robert Service who wrote about them. One of his verses goes like this:

> There's a race of men that can't fit in,
> A race that can't stay still;
> For they break the hearts of kith and kin
> And they roam the world at will.
> They roam the fields and race the floods
> And climb the mountain's crest,
> For theirs is the curse of the gypsy's blood
> And they don't know when to rest.
> If each man could find his groove
> What a deep mark he would make

But he chops and changes and each fresh move
Is only a fresh mistake.
Ha! Ha! he is one of the Legion's lost!
He was never meant to win;
He's a rolling stone and it's bred in the bone:
He's a man that can't fit in.

Tommy was in on the *Queen Elizabeth*'s secret launching in the early part of the war and her record is legendary. She was 85,000 tons and it is said that as a troopship she carried as many as 16,000 troops at one go. Her speed was top secret and she contributed a lot to the war effort. Anyway, Tommy told me to meet him in London, I think it was at Euston Station, and he took me to his home in Balham. On the way he told me his wife was expecting her first child and I was embarrassed, for we didn't talk like that back home. In any case, we had them by the dozen, so it was nothing new. I was now just nineteen but for all my experience up to then, I was still as thick as two short planks in the ways of the world. The first thing Tommy did was to get the Harris tweed suit off me and fit me out in a midnight blue gaberdine suit, bought in Savile Row with hand-stitched collar, then all the rage. Tommy had a dozen or more, suits, I mean, and as for ties I thought he owned a shop there were so many, all with big splashy colours from Bond's on Broadway, New York. They strike me as vulgar now – but then one acquires a wee bit of taste as one goes along, eh?

After meeting Kathleen, his wife, who incidentally came from Cashel in Tipperary, I was taken on a fast tour around the high spots of London. Somehow there must be a lot of Tommy in me, for I have the same rush through life as he. 'That's the Guildhall; that's Table Mountain. This is Times Square' – you know everything in a hurry! A couple of days later we set sail – on the train, I mean – for Southampton, 'the gateway to

England', where all the big passenger liners docked. The *Queen Elizabeth*, *Queen Mary*, *Mauretania*, *Britannic*, *Ascania* and *Aquitania*, and a host of others – all over 35,000 tons or so – looked quite impressive as they sailed, not all at one time, mind you, up the Solent to berth.

The *Lizzy* and the *Mary*, as they were affectionately known, were over 80,000 tons and their business was the American passenger and specialised cargo trade across the Atlantic (known to seamen as the Western Ocean). South America was covered by the Royal Mail line, Australasia by the P & O (Pacific and Orient) and South Africa by the Castle line, whose boats were called after famous castles – *Capetown Castle*, *Bloemfontein Castle*, *Windsor Castle*, to name a few. The *Windsor Castle* was the scene of a murder about this time. It seems one of the bedroom stewards got himself involved in a shipboard romance with a young actress and it went wrong, so he murdered her and pushed her body out through the porthole somewhere near the Canary Islands. I sailed on her sister ship the *Capetown Castle* and it was all the talk.

As you can see, the oceans were well covered with ships. The ones I mentioned belonged to British companies; there were American, Dutch, Scandinavian, German and French lines as well. I don't want to bore you with too much shipping but I feel it's a must to give an idea of what Southampton was like at that time. The war wasn't long over and travel restrictions had just been lifted; Europe was just reopened to all the European ethnic groups coming back to visit the 'old country'. The Atlantic Ocean was as busy as the English Channel – at one time reputed to be the busiest stretch of water in the world – for flying hadn't really got off the ground yet (!) and shipping never had it so good. When you walked up the gangway of one of those big liners you entered a new world, something you would never get over. Excuse me now, for I'm talking about first and second class; sad to say, third class was different as most of their cabins were below the waterline. Space was tight and for a first-time traveller it could be quite claustrophobic. On top of that, in the busy season you might be asked to share a cabin. As the voyage to New York took five days, fifteen hours, if you had to share with the wrong person it could be quite upsetting.

In Southampton my cousin Tommy took me round the shipping offices and the seaman's union which I had to join before any shipping company would even look at me. The union was a closed shop (don't ask me what that means, for I never did get it explained) but I got a job as a dishwasher on the *Aquitania* (50,000-odd tons), sailing to Halifax, Nova Scotia. I tearfully said goodbye to Tommy at the foot of the gangway as he was about to sail away to New York on the *Queen Elizabeth*.

Once again I was on my own, a total stranger in a whole new world but I pulled myself together and made my way up the gangway to start the greatest adventure of my life. I didn't realise that the world I had learned about at the Christian Brothers' would become a reality to me and would eventually shrink in size. Funny how things stand out in your mind, a song, show or person, and at that time a song came out called 'Faraway Places'. It went something like this:

Those faraway places with the strange sounding names,
    faraway over the sea,
Those faraway places with the strange sounding names
    are calling, calling me.
Going to China, or even Siam, I'm gonna see for
    myself
Those faraway places with the strange sounding names
In a book that I took from the shelf . . .

Little did I realise at that first step onto the deck of the *Aquitania* that I would be living those words for the next ten years of my life.

Ships ferried back and forth from Southampton to New York, like the two big *Queens* and the *Mauretania*, whilst the *Britannic* and *Ascania* ferried to Boston and Toronto. The *Aquitania* took seven days to sail to Halifax, with two days there and a seven-day return to Southampton for a further two days. On the way out and on the way back there would be a five-hour call at Cherbourg or Le Harve to pick up or drop off passengers for Europe. As Royal Mail ships, they would also be expected to pick up mail. I used to look forward to this stop, for we took on freshly caught Dover Sole for passenger consumption. Since I was working in the kitchen I got my share, and I can tell you with tartar sauce no fish tasted better; it was always on the last menu of the trip. The *Aquitania* was built in 1917 after the style of the *Titanic*, with a high superstructure, four big funnels painted black, red and white just like the other ships of the fleet – Cunard White Star, I mean. One of my lasting memories of her was the creaking night and day. When I asked an old salt about this his reply was, 'When she stops creaking get off her!'

As I was saying, I got a job in the first-class platehouse washing up, and, God, I never knew people could use so many dishes for one meal. After a while, I helped my eight partners to dump the dirty plates out the porthole. Now, I'm not proud of this but it seemed the thing to do at the time, for the plates would come in that fast and numerous that we found it hard to keep up. If it were possible to walk on the bottom of the ocean from Southampton to New York there would be a path of plates, cutlery, glass and silverware, all the way. There was a great air of affluence around and wastage seemed to go hand in hand with it.

The route to Halifax is in the North Atlantic and since my first trip was in the month of March I can tell you it was no mill-pond; we pitched and rolled the whole way, day and night for seven days. To put it mildly, I was seasick, and I was sick of the sea as well. For the uninitiated, when a ship pitches, she goes down nose first into the waves and her stern or rear end comes up out of the water. Try walking in such conditions when the waves are fifty or sixty feet high. When she pitched, the deck came up to meet you or dropped away from you, most uncomfortable, to say the least. To go up on deck was a hazard on its own, for the ship was really steaming on and what with the gales blowing, it would have been easy to have been swept overboard. There was some days that we didn't see daylight at all.

This was in the days before stabilisers became standard but now all the big ships have them so I reckon it must be more relaxing. Rolling was another kettle of fish. She would swing from side to side and sometimes you'd think she was never going to straighten up again. You'd have to stop walking and wait for the thing to come back to the perpendicular. It was funny to see everybody standing at an angle of from 30° to 60°. When a storm rose, all the moveable furniture was screwed to the deck and 'fiddles', or little sides about two inches high, were put on the tables to keep the plates and condiments from slipping off onto a passenger's lap. I learned later when I became a waiter to pour water on the tablecloth and that kept everything in place.

Well, we arrived in Halifax and I can remember debating with myself whether to go back or not. I had been miserably seasick and to face another seven days of it was nothing to look forward to; on that journey out you could smell the icebergs that were just over the horizon. Still, there was nothing else for it but to go back, for I had even thought of joining the mounties but they either hadn't a hat big enough or a horse wee enough, so I settled for homeward bound and the same gruelling job. Anyway, I had to tell all my pals at home where I'd been and show off a bit.

On arrival in Southampton I felt at home but the ground kept coming up to meet me and it took a day ashore to get back on an even keel again. As for the passengers, I never saw one of them either outward- nor inward-bound, so I can't make comment. I signed up for another trip – I forgot to tell you I was a glutton. This was no better but I was getting my sea legs and it stood to me in the future. I made that second trip, enjoyed it no more than I expected and I decided I'd had enough of Halifax and the western ocean. I took myself down to the Union Castle Line and signed on as a a first-class waiter on the *Capetown Castle*, calling at Capetown, Durban, East London and Port Elizabeth. The round trip took six weeks, including a stop at Tenerife in the Canaries. Here we picked up the mail; most ships afloat in those days were Royal Mail ships, consequently their names were prefixed RMS like RMS *Capetown Castle*, etc. My wage incidentally was £7.10s a month all found, set by agreement with the Board of Trade and the seaman's union. It applied to all seamen irrespective of the company.

As a waiter I was now in a position to earn tips. That sounds OK but we were dealing with two kinds of people here, one was the 'awfully awfully' English, still bluffing their way round the dwindling Empire, living out of each other's pockets – and couldn't tip their waiter. The second was the South African – the Yarpy – who didn't know how to tip: they were used to their houseboys running and fetching. I found them gross indeed.

You might wonder how I got the job as first-class waiter – well I chanced my arm, as, I suppose, 80 per cent of those around me were doing too. The menu was a simple four- or five-course plate-service with a couple of things each to chose from. With sixteen people to take care of, the more fingers you had the more plates you could carry, and if you were a juggler that helped too. Now and again when you had your complement of plates complete with dinners and the fingers of your carrying arm playing a violin concerto on the bottoms of the hot plates, one of the cooks would hand you an even hotter one and scald the hand off you. In the heat of the moment and with all the aggro going on around you it was not funny; so one night at dinner this wise guy of a cook handed me a hot one and I distinctly saw the grin on his face – he knew what he done all right – but he didn't reckon on what was to happen next, for I split him with every plate I had in my hands, all seven of them. And into the bargain, when he ran to the other side of the big kitchen, I followed him and between his own blood and the gravy, slices of roast beef, mashed potatoes, bits of fish hanging from him, he was a sorry sight and, I houl' ye, he never tried that trick again. I was brought before the chief steward who knew the score all right and 'by the way' got a severe warning. It was the most they could do to me, for this sort of thing was going on and I had brought it to a head for them.

Morning and afternoon tea was served on deck and I can tell you now that the punters never missed a meal. Still, for all that, the voyage was beautiful, for after just one night at sea, travelling south out of Southampton, we woke to the sun shining down on us from a clear blue sky and it was here that we changed into our whites. The normal uniform was a navy blue serge suit and in the heat of the kitchen and dining room it could be quite uncomfortable. The whites were more suitable for the tropics. The time between meals – breakfast, lunch and dinner – was our own but as there is so little to do at sea we read, wrote home or went up on deck to sunbathe. It was heaven sailing along the west coast of Africa and across the equator, where we had the 'crossing-the-line' ceremony. At this point some of the officers dressed up as Father Neptune, welcoming the passengers in to his domain and with the help of some stewardesses dressed as mermaids he would dunk them in the pool and present each of them with a 'crossing-the-line' certificate. It was all good fun and I wonder how many of these certificates are treasured in trinket boxes today with memories of fifty years ago.

The Castle boats were all passenger/cargo ships, so we had plenty of deck space on the hatches both to sunbathe during the day and sleep out at night, as the crew cabins were quite stuffy. The crew quarters were usually below the waterline, so it was like being in a submarine with the sound of fresh air blowing down into the cabin all night. After a time you got used to it and tried to ignore it, but it all boiled down to the crew's being the last consideration of the company. It surely was the days of 'iron ships and wooden men'. Still, I was young and like most of my shipmates we accepted it. A bunch of us would mark out our sleeping spot on the deck for night and it was soothing to be lulled to sleep with the gentle swish of the water splashing against the for'ard end as she sliced her way south. Since she wasn't a cruising ship her speed was always flat out, for deadlines had to be met.

During the day the sailfish and porpoise would accompany us and play games with us and I could have watched them for hours bouncing off the sides. Older men there said that they were rubbing the lice off themselves, but sure your guess is as good as mine. Shoals of flying fish would pass us by as well and I used to think they were wee cheats, bluffing us into thinking they could fly when really they couldn't. They just propelled themselves out of the water, spread their fins and looked like they were flying.

About five days out we called into Funchal in Madeira. There was no docking space, so we anchored off and all the bumboats came out to meet us. Nowadays travellers miss a lot of the excitement when flying into another country. Everything is so sophisticated at airports: you land, go through customs and emigration and are bustled into a taxi to your hotel. It lacks the atmosphere and the thrill of seeing a new country and its people from a ship. The mail was swung out in the usual rope slings and placed into a smaller boat that came alongside to deliver the customs and emigration officials who came aboard to check the ships' logs – in our case, I'm sure, just a formality – and then the crew and passengers were allowed ashore for a couple of hours. The chatter going on between the natives in the bumboats and the passengers and crew left on board was unbelievable and I was to hear it many times after in my future trips around the world. In the Caribbean, all around the continent of South America, out in Java, Bali, Hong Kong and through the islands of the South Pacific the same trading went on, people just selling their homemade, handmade crafts, basketware, carvings, paintings and light pottery.

In Funchal that day we traded soap for walkie-talkie dolls, for soap was a great commodity. I could have given them all the soap they needed when I was at school, for I didn't have a great conceit in it but times had changed and now it was being used as barter. The passengers threw coins into the water and the wee natives would dive in from their own boats and catch them before they sank too deep. We could see all the underwater action from our deck, for the water was crystal clear and a blue colour from the sky. Oil disasters were unheard of, so pollution was nil and it was sheer magic. Half a dozen older native men would be allowed to climb up to the ship's bridge, which was about eighty to a hundred feet above the waterline – where the captain – or God (you know, I swear he thought he was) – had his quarters and from there they would dive off altogether, like swallows in flight. After about eight or ten hours we pushed on south to the Cape of Good Hope and Capetown.

I'll never forget that first sight of Capetown and Table Mountain. What a spectacle, sailing into one of the nicest harbours I have ever been in. Since docking or arrival times always seemed to be early mornings, there was no better time to see Capetown with its backdrop of Table Mountain taking its night blanket of mist off for the day and to see and hear the hustle and bustle of the natives setting up gangways for passengers, cargo, and last of all crew. It was thrilling, for whilst I had seen plenty of coloured men in Derry with the Yanks, these men looked really primitive. Gangs of them gathered together ready to go down into the various hatches dressed only in breechclouts with all kinds of tribal markings on their faces and bodies and noses, and ears pierced with coloured sticks. Each hatch had its own witchdoctor and chanter who chanted all day long to keep the men at work and I can tell you, for a first-timer like myself it was frightening.

Then there was an old, old black man with white, white hair in the Union Castle uniform who came on board and went straight to the captain to deliver personal mail from the shore office and he had the honour of being the first man to step on board even before customs and emigration. This old fellow, his name was Snowball (your guess is as good as mine!) had been doing this for a hundred years or more. Well, it probably seemed like that, but it was a long time and this, I was told, was his last trip. He died shortly after we sailed but I'm glad I saw him, for he was one of the gems in life's trinket box. I was informed that the company gave him a seaman's funeral and took his corpse out to sea for burial with full honours. Wasn't that nice? I think the sea has lovely traditions. That's wrong, I know, but you know I mean the men who sail her.

The hatch covers were taken off and the crews of native workers would descend down into the holds to empty cargo and fill up with other cargo for a new destination. Now, all this was before television, so I can tell you it was pretty fascinating. The older hands said a lot of them were just down from the kraals to earn enough to buy a wife and they had to live outside

111

the town limits at night. The laws were so bad there that a white male could not even ask a coloured female directions in the street under the threat of jail, so while things are more relaxed now, improvement has been long overdue. Capetown itself is a beautiful port, clean and tidy, but at the time I write about, it wouldn't have been my choice to settle in for the laws were too depressing.

Three days later I was glad to say farewell to Capetown when at sundown she returned the compliment with Table Mountain putting on her tablecloth or blanket for the night. I'm sure she did not have us in mind, for she's been doing it since time began. We sailed out of one of the most beautiful harbours in the world with the sun fighting to keep its place in the day, only to lose again to night and the moon. We started up the east coast to the other three ports in the itinerary: Durban, East London and Port Elizabeth, where the hustle and bustle was the same and only the scenery differed; but they couldn't match Capetown.

With two days in each port we did a lot of swimming in beaches, where no natives were allowed and this to my mind was nothing short of cruel since it was their land or at least they were there before the white man. Sorry I couldn't change anything. We called into Capetown again on the way home and loaded up a cargo of fruit, peaches, grapes and bananas for England and then started the two-week sail back to South-ampton. I made a second trip down to the Cape and I thought that I'd seen the last of it but I returned on another ship the following year and that was even more exciting.

HOME IS THE SAILOR...

On arrival in Southampton I noticed that the *Queen Mary* was lying alongside. I went to the Cunard office and was lucky enough to get back into the company as a dishwasher. We sailed for New York and the weather was a lot better as it was summertime but contrary to the song, the living wasn't easy – we worked fourteen hours a day, because the ship was packed both ways, going and coming. What came over had to go back. The trip took four days, fifteen hours, and she was on time. When the *Queen* arrived off the Statue of Liberty and started her stately 'walk' up the Hudson river to her berth (or for the record, 'throne') at Pier 90 North River she was greeted by all the other ships and barges with klaxon horns blowing and fire hoses spraying water. It was really a sight to behold and this sort of treatment was accorded her till her last voyage out of New York, many years later.

Dockland the world over is the same, for the same routine has to be done. If it's a big passenger liner like one of the *Queens*, first the pilot meets her outside the harbour or channel and takes over the control of the ship at that point and is responsible to the company and Lloyd's, until she is tied up safely at berth. He then steps down and gives command back to the skipper. The skipper can override the pilot but if he does the responsibility falls back on the company. It happened one time a couple of years later, when the longshoremen came out on strike in sympathy with some other crowd – you never know who. Anyway, the pilot came on, paid his respects, probably got a feed of drink and stated his position: there was nobody to tie up the ship. The captain took her up the river himself. I almost forgot to mention the tugs, for they where an integral part of the whole setup, as it took six tugs to manoeuvre the ship into the berth.

Now, if you can imagine a sow pig lying with all her wee piglets feeding round her, that's what the *Queen Mary* looked like. She was 82,000 tons and each tug was about 500 tons but it was a delight to see them push and shove her into position and I loved watching all their antics with the six of them working together as one. They were owned by a company called Moran, all had girls' names, were painted red and black and silver, and I swear you could eat your dinner off the deck they were so clean. I remember one day coming back on board and on one of the tugs tied up alongside, a deckhand was repairing ropes, or whatever sailors do, so I thought I'd be smart and says,

'Would you bring me back a monkey?' and without breaking his stride he says, 'Aye, one just like you.' I thought it very quick indeed.

Let's get back to the pilot and the captain. The captain kept command and took the ship up the river, amidst all the fanfare: horns blazing, fireboats deluging water everywhere, while the traffic stopped along the Twelfth Avenue overhead highway and tooted their horns. Even the men on strike clapped and cheered as the big ship nosed her way under her own steam up the river and shelved in at right angles. It was indeed a great feat of navigation for the tides run very strong on the North River but again sad to say it was all for naught, for I'm told it lost him his commodoreship. He was due to take over the *Queen Elizabeth* as commodore of the fleet next voyage but I think the company may have been rebuked by Lloyd's of London for risking the welfare of the ship. See what you get for doing a good turn! Or was it showing off, in his case?

The Manhattan skyline just has to be seen, and from the sea or river. It is really impressive with its skyscrapers seemingly doing just that, and I'm sure it is even more so at present; my last trip was in 1961 over thirty years ago. (I've seen only one other place to match it, though I'm sure there are more, and that was São Paulo in Brazil.) Manhattan's avenues run lengthways along the island and these are crossed at right angles by the streets; it's a great system and you would be hard pushed to get lost. We docked, as I said, at Pier 90 between 48th and 49th Street at Twelfth Avenue and to get to the streets from the pier we had to cross under the Twelfth Avenue highway, a freeway that allowed cars and trucks to bypass the city or let them drop into it where they wished. (Maybe 'drop' is an unfortunate choice of word!) It was really something to see, though I guess it's common enough now in all countries, but all those years ago it was like something out of Flash Gordon.

It took a wee while to get used to the cars coming at you from the wrong side of the street and more than once I had a scare and a barrage of insults and curses from a New York cab driver. As soon as I got finished on board I was away with myself, a proper tourist with my mouth open, flabbergasted at the sights, walking up 49th Street across Eleventh, Tenth and Ninth Avenues. (These three were known as Hell's Kitchen. I mention this because in my early boxing days I had read about the famous Jack Johnson and Battling Siki being stabbed to death there. I suppose it was as sore a place as any to get stabbed!) Then on to Eighth, Seventh, Sixth and Fifth Avenues and so on across town to the East Side, where I imagined I would see the Dead End Kids I had imitated so much a few short years before in the Midland picture house. Standing here in the heart of it, I felt I was really in dreamland, only Cagney, Mugsy and Sachs didn't show up.

Despite the old saying, I stood in Times Square at different times, but though it was crowded I didn't see one person from home. I felt very lonely as I looked into people's faces looking for a nod of recognition. I always thought it was the loneliest place in the world, where people don't just ignore you but would walk over you. It's very sad indeed, but I loved it. The Big Apple is without doubt the greatest city in the world, for there is everything you want in it. That first day on my way up 49th Street I heard a shot and looking down Ninth Avenue, I saw a negro fall and a cop running up to him with his gun out and it transpires the fellow was running along the street and the cop called him to stop and whether he didn't hear him or not I don't know, but the cop shot him – in the leg – another sore place. After seeing that, I could feel the adrenalin start to flow. Don't forget, it was pre-1968 before shooting in the North became fashionable. I made my way on up 49th Street to Broadway, still with my mouth open, and what do you think?

but a middle-aged woman fell at my feet. This is where the walking-over-you bit comes in to play, for there she was lying on the sidewalk and everybody just kept on walking past. I went over to assist her and they nearly walked over me too. It took a while before the traffic cop left the middle of the road to come to both her and my assistance but I got a good lesson on survival that day. If you're going to collapse anywhere, don't do it in New York.

One of the first places I looked up was Jack Dempsey's bar. Here Jack would sit holding court and shake your hand or autograph anything you gave him from a twenty dollar bill up. He was a great character, one of the all-time greats in boxing. Above the bar there was this huge picture about twenty feet by thirty feet of him knocking out Jess Willard, a mountain of a man, all of six foot six to Jack's five foot eleven. Close by was another famous bar owned by another legendary boxer who was also my idol: Mickey Walker, ex-world middleweight champ, known as the 'Toy Bulldog'. I remember being in there about five years later with my cousin Tommy when a black nun came in begging. She had the whole regalia on her, a huge set of rosary beads round her waist and she really looked the part but when the barman spotted her, he used bad language to her and proceeded to throw her out. I got on my high horse and reach-ed for the barman. I was scandalised, but Tommy restrained me saying she was a phoney. Another lesson in the university of life.

42nd Street, with Times Square, was known in vaudeville days as Tin Pan Alley but even at that time (the early fifties) the songs from the shows were plugged day and night, for New York never slept, except the bums who dossed over the air ducts of the underground and the skyscrapers above. For all its wealth New York had its share of poverty. I could go on and on about New York but I'll have to move on a bit.

I did the summer season, from April to September, on the

Queen Mary and I was allowed home on leave. I really looked forward to it, most of all to get showing off to my pals and telling them of my travels, to name-drop a few big cities that to most of them were only wee dots on the map. Nowadays with the advent of universal flight the world has shrunk considerably and working-class people like myself can go to places that once we could only dream about. Well, to travel back to Derry from Southampton took a three-hour train journey to London, ten hours in a train to Heysham, twelve hours overnight on a boat to Belfast and, best of all, the two-hour train to Derry. When I hear jokes about British Rail I can say surely, 'I was there', for I can still remember the woman pouring tea in Heysham Station at 4 o'clock in the morning and she was poetry in motion. Picture a hundred thick British Rail teacups sitting on the counter, all sugared and milked (God knows how long beforehand) and a woman with a two-gallon teapot just spraying the whole lot. To crown it out, the one and only teaspoon was chained to the table by a three-foot length of chain. I'm only sorry I didn't have a pair of nippers on me, for I would like to have sabotaged the whole catering project at Heysham docks.

The boat from Heysham to Belfast and back was to me a nightmare, for it was run as if the travellers were cattle and the crew did everything but wallop you up the gangway. Numbers didn't matter, as there were not enough bunks or cabins anyway, and with everybody being sick on top of each other the stench of vomit was all over the place. Conditions on the Heysham boat were truly grim. The shipping company blamed it on the war but sure the war was over four or five years. Anything was good enough for the Paddies. I'll never forget coming home after my first complete tour of the world and meeting some of the Derry lads who were coming back home from England. As they all knew me they started asking me about where I was – as if I wasn't going to tell them anyway! – so I started dropping names like Australia, China, Brazil, you know, here and there, and they were all ears. The crack was good, the ropes were cast off fore and aft and I was seasick before we left the harbour wall. I often wondered what those fellows thought about me, but that was how the Heysham boat affected me.

I was slightly disappointed when I got off the train in Derry, for I thought the wee town closed down after I left, six months previous. But no, life seemed to have gone on as usual. The taximen, all of whom I knew, gathered round to hear where I'd been. This was not unusual for me, for when I would come back in the morning after a fight in Belfast they would all call to me, 'Red, how did you do?' and I would modestly say, 'Ah it was OK; he was easy. I knocked him out in the first or third . . .' or whatever round it was, and they always wished me luck. Well, on this occasion my suitcases were plastered with different first-class hotel labels from around the world, as was the custom of travellers in those days, so I took a taxi just up the street about 400 yards. Sounds blasé but I had a load of presents and two suitcases, a gaberdine suit, buckle shoes, white socks and a tie so flashy you could light your fag from it. Boy, I cut a quare dash or I thought I did! God how times change.

This puts me in mind of a fellow I knew from Wellington Street – we'll call him Harry so's not to embarrass him. Well, he went to England to work and after three months he decided to come home and as he was approaching the bottom of Wellington Street he called some wee lad playing about and gave him half a crown to show him where he lived. I felt a wee bit like Harry that day.

THE ONLY GIRL
IN THE WORLD

I think it's about time I introduced Agnes Clarke, the girl who was to become my wife. The Waterside Boys' Club ran socials or dances at the weekends, average age, fourteen to seventeen years and while they were attended by the local youth of the parish, people from other parishes across the town were welcomed. It was at one of these socials that I saw Agnes for the first time and though I wasn't exactly Fred Astaire I nevertheless asked her out for a dance and during it I enquired all about her:

her name, who she was and above all where she lived. This part was very important, for if I had to walk her home, there was no sense in walking a marathon. The idea was to get a girl living close by and Agnes suited the criterion in this matter. I asked to walk her home but she told me she was with her sister and two other pals but if I wanted to tag along, I could. To take the bare look off it I rustled up a couple of my pals and we all walked home together.

I thought Agnes and her sister Vera were very alike for they both had long wavy hair and were the same height (about five feet two inches) and very pretty but Vera died aged twenty-one with leukaemia just before Agnes and I got married. It was a terrible blow to the family, and at the time of her death, members of the Long Tower parish were on pilgrimage to Lourdes, so they were all praying for her. She was very funny and quick with her answers. I know she would have made a good sister-in-law.

I'll always remember my first real date with Agnes. I was to meet her at the junction of Fountain Street and Bishop Street at 8 pm, and there was I, dressed like a tailor's dummy, face and hair shining, as nervous as a bag of cats, with my box of Milk Tray chocolates under my arm, when up Bishop Street came this bunch of girls with Agnes amongst them. She was taking no chances of being stood up, hence the backup, and that night we went to the second house in the Palace, which was over at 11 pm. We stopped in at Battisti's ice-cream parlour and had a milk shake and then made our way home.

I was embarrassed walking out with Agnes at first, because at this time I was just starting to box and people recognised me or at least I thought they did. I didn't think it right that a boxer should go with girls, for some of the old men in the gym were always preaching to me that women and boxing don't mix. God, I had a lot to learn but I never did get the hang of it. We stood along the wall up at the Mrs Alexander Memorial Cottages in New Street – still there, thank God, though New Street is gone now, sad to say – and since it was then coming up to 11.30 pm it was time to say goodnight. No definite date was arranged for the future but we both knew we would see each other up the town the next night and that's how it all started. After a month or two at this, dating a couple of times a week, I was introduced to Mr and Mrs Clarke and got my feet under the table.

Mr Clarke was a nice grey-haired middle-aged man still able to do a day's work in the nearby foundry, where he worked as a moulder. This would have been a heavy physical job but he was one of the old stock and worked till he could do no more. For the short little time I knew him I liked him very much. He was like what a father *should* look like and now and again I see someone like him in an ad on television for bread. I never heard a cross word out of him, although Vera, Agnes and Nellie must have taken one or two out of him. (I'm just kidding here, for I'm sure that they came under Mrs Clarke's management.) I was away on a world cruise when Mr Clarke died very suddenly on Christmas Day, 1954, the year our eldest child Marina was born. I wish I could have had more time with him as he would have had so much more to tell me. God rest him.

Mrs Clarke was a busy wee woman, a great neighbour, always there at everyone's beck and call, and I can still see her tripping with her wee short steps down to Annie's corner shop two doors away for the daily groceries. By the way, Annie's is still there although the whole surrounding district has been re-developed and a rumour has been circulating that one of the big multinationals was negotiating a takeover. (As my grandson would say, 'Just a joke, Granda.') Mrs Clarke, or Dotty as she was known – nothing dotty about her – was the same height as Agnes and wore a flowered crossover coat-apron. Her hair was usually in a plait tied up in a bun at the back of her head and she had a nice short quick step. I suppose this was from her very tiny feet of which she was proud. She never interfered in our married life but was always there to help us out in difficult times, above and beyond the call of duty – like the time when we came back from America and had no home, she took us in. That is Agnes, myself, Marina aged five, Giovanni four, Fionnbarr three, Adian two and Siobhán an infant. It was a big undertaking but she did it and I think on her every day in my prayers.

Our courtship was a long one, when you come to think of it, for when I first met Agnes we were both about sixteen or seventeen but we didn't get married until we were twenty-three. That seems a long time but I was in the Free State army, over in England and away at sea during all this. We took it for granted that we were for each other and not a lot of conscious thought went into it. I can tell you there were no third parties involved! We wrote to each other nearly every day and spent all our time together whenever I came home on leave.

Coming back to Mr and Mrs Clarke, I must have done all right for I soon got the use of the wee front porch and this augured well for me, as the old gateway at the hatchery could be draughty enough. Number 9 New Street was one of a terrace of eleven houses with a kitchen dining-room and back hall leading out to the backyard where the toilet and running water was. Upstairs consisted of two bedrooms and that was it and the only difference between that and my own house was that we had an attic. But the happiness that came out of that wee house couldn't be measured by any earthly standards. That was forty-eight years ago and I can honestly say nobody has ever come between us, in all my travels. Agnes has always been and always will be *numero uno*. We are now in our forty-first year of married life and we have always tried to do things together. Agnes has been a steadying hand to me, although I don't make that too public, for she might rise above her station. Seriously though, she has always been there for advice when I needed her.

We had been going steady for a year when I decided to go to sea but as I've already said I always kept in touch and wrote nearly every day. After a couple of years' sailing, during one of my cruises we called at Dun Laoghaire and I invited Agnes and my family up to see the ship with all the millionaire Yanks. It was there that I proposed. We both took things for granted, so it was only a matter of setting the date, but being a seaman, I had to get a special clearance from the bishop, in case I was already married to some Balinese go-go dancer or Ubangi maiden in Basutoland or somewhere. After the investigation I got my clearance papers and we got married that 10 August and our first child Marina was born on 11 August. (I hasten to add it was a year later.) I'd just come home from a visit to Mexico and it being the Marian year, we called her Marina. About eighteen months later I was in Naples and our second child, a son, was born, so rather than have a Big John and a Wee John, or as the Yanks would say, John Senior and John Junior, we called him Giovanni.

Then Fionnbarr was born and guess where I was then? Cork. Fionnbarr, I am sorry to say, died a very sudden death. He was only a few months newly married to Frances and they were expecting their first child. You could say they had the world at their feet when the tragedy struck. That was in 1985 and the family, and I'm sure I speak also for Frances and their son Paul Fionnbarr, will never get over that.

After Fionnbarr came Adian, who was called for a nun I knew in South Africa. Sister Phelim was called Aideen Morrison before taking her vows and her father owned the big shop in Duke Street which I mentioned earlier, the one with all the toys and drapery. Mr Morrison knew all of our family – the

Waterside was very parochial – and on hearing that I would be calling into Capetown, he gave me Aideen's address. Before Pope John, some missionary orders went abroad to teach the gospel, never to come home again, and this was one of those cases. I can remember her asking me to try to get through to her mother that she wouldn't be coming back again as that was her calling. She was a lovely girl, a teacher, and when she took me into her class all the wee coloured children stood up and said in a well-rehearsed choir, 'Good morning'. It brought back memories of the times at my own school when we would all be asked to stand up whenever some stranger entered the room. She got into a flat spin when she found out I'd walked up to the school myself from the docks, for this was District 6, notorious for violence and murder. When I was ready to go back to the ship she made me call a taxi for safety. Thank God for Pope John, for he released them of their vows and I am glad to say I met Sister Phelim in Belfast some years later, but she has since returned to South Africa. That's dedication for you. I met her brother in the Philippines the following year.

Adian was born in Los Angeles and has since claimed her American citizenship. She is married and lives in Los Angeles with her husband and son. On the morning she was born I nearly got a ticket for speeding but when the young cop who pulled me down saw the predicament I was in or rather the predicament Adian was in, he sent us on our way, wishing us the best of luck. We all moved back to Derry and a little later Siobhán was born. Siobhán watches every move I make and she has me spoiled, for if I only look at something or other she buys it for me. She's a gem. Last but not least came Ciaran and at this time in my life I was in behind a nine-foot chainlink fence in Du Pont's chemical plant at Maydown, trapped, I thought, for the rest of my life. Ciaran married a wee girl from Donegal and they have a son Rudi, a likable wee rogue.

Agnes and myself have had a good married life up to the present, although she hasn't enjoyed the best of health. We had moved to Strathfoyle, a little housing estate primarily built for Du Pont workers, and Agnes suffered a slipped disc. That was over thirty-four years ago and it has dogged her ever since. She is in constant pain but if you met her and asked her how she was she would say, 'grand', but I know different. For all that, she has been behind me all the way and threw in her full support in whatever I took on. I only had to mention something and she backed me and gave me all the help she could. We tried a couple of things together but the hardest was running a fish-and-chip mobile van.

The hours were long and late but Agnes was with me and many a wee burn she got with the hot oil in the fryer. The first van we bought was called the Jolly Fryer and there was a painting on the back of it of a wee monk frying chips and a clatter of other monks waiting with their plates. It was very appropriate but the only thing was when we went to the Field on the Glorious Twelfth we had to make sure to have the van well backed up to the hedge so that no one would get behind and see this wee monk. There is nothing surer than if he was spotted we would have been burned out, so there was no sense in taking chances. After putting a good dash of salt on the fish and chips I would pass them over to Agnes and say, 'Put a drop of salt in those.' So she would salt them too and then Marina would ask them if they would like some salt and vinegar on them, so by this time the fish and chips were well salted. There's more than one way to skin a cat.

THEY ALSO SERVE...

I had been washing dishes on the *Queen Mary* for about three months when a new second steward arrived in charge. As it turned out he was an ex-boxing champ of Australia called Tommy Aymer. He took a shine to me and asked me if I'd like a change of job. I was delighted, so I replied, 'Yeah sure', and he says, 'Where do you want to go?' I says, 'Into the first-class dining-room', and he says, 'OK, get your uniform in Southampton.' Well, as soon as we hit the beach, I was up to Baker's, the naval outfitters, for a uniform. Up till then I was just a dishwasher, so I only required white coats and cook's checked trousers. I guess they saw a greenhorn coming, for I was sold three of this, four of that and six of the other. I didn't need half of the gear and some of it I have never ever worn. I came back on board and reported to the first-class dining-room dressed like a wee penguin with my stiff front, dickey bow, tuxedo and trousers with a silk stripe down them.

About here I have to tell you about the shoes. Baker's was an old firm and naturally they had accumulated a lot of old stock over the years, so I bought a pair of the regulation black navy shoes, fitted them on and left the shop. Everything went fine: I got all dickied up and had my first white stiff front on with the white bow tie, tied first class – not that I would say it myself – and headed up to the dining-room to serve my first meal. I should have checked the shoes a wee bit more but as long as they fitted me I was happy enough, that is until I started to walk in them but by then it was too late: the ship had sailed and I was scuppered. At the arch of the sole a bit of stitching came undone with age, and the old shoes creaked and screeched with every step I took. It really was a scream – if you'll forgive the pun. As I walked up and down the dining-room floor the scrunching was terrible. You could see the diners stop talking and turn round to see what was coming and do you know, it was the nearest thing to Stan Laurel I ever got. The head waiter followed me out to the kitchen and blew a fuse. I had all the waiters and cooks in screeches too, and even though it was a serious time in my life I enjoyed it. The cure was funnier, for I had to stand in the scuppers and soak my shoes in the water. The scuppers are the drains around the kitchen and there is always a couple of inches of water in them. This went on every meal until I got to New York, where I made a beeline to the nearest shoe shop, and bought myself a proper pair.

I'll never forget the first day; it was a nightmare. I got my station, a large round table for eight and was told to set up for dinner. I could have done an appendicectomy easier. You know, I never knew people needed as many pieces of silver to eat their meals and, where I was content with the old spoon at home, these people needed no less than twelve pieces each. That number would have done my whole family. The world is ill-divided. I'll let you figure out where the twelve pieces were set yourself. There were also three glasses per person to go on the table and all this time I'm watching round the rest of the room to see what every other waiter is doing and trying to do the same.

The passengers were all on board and away we sailed for New York. She was loaded to the gills, all three classes, first, second, third or tourist, sometimes known as steerage in other lines. It doesn't matter now, for by this time I was ready to jump overboard, only I realised I couldn't swim. The passengers or 'bloods' started to come into the dining-room and I was standing by my table in a bundle of nerves waiting on them. I pulled out all the gents' chairs and sat the ladies in theirs, took their wraps or whatever had to be taken and then the pantomime, or should I say pandemonium, started. First the menu was in culinary French, so I hadn't a clue what they were on about; second, when I did get all the order written down where the blazes do I get the stuff? The kitchen was so big and each course had its own corner. I was completely at sea in every sense of the word. I struggled through on the outward trip but with every meal I was getting in deeper. I had bitten off more than I could chew.

On the homeward voyage, two days out of New York, Tommy Aymer, who had given me my chance – or should I say, got me into this fix – took me into his office and said, 'I'm going to give you a change and I know you'll be mad at me now. But you'll thank me in years to come. I'm putting you up to the engineers' mess where you'll get to know the food properly.' That was twice in my life I was taken off the job. First in the Free State army – when I was drummed out – and now in the first-class dining-room on the *Queen Mary*. I took the change and reported to the engineers' mess, which was made up of tradesmen – electricians, plumbers, carpenters, fitters, mechanics and such, and because of their trade, they carried one, two, or two and a half gold bands round their cuffs which made them officers and entitled to the first-class menu. There were 120 of them and it's no wonder the company went bust for they were accorded too many privileges. At sea they looked down on the stewards but it was just plain jealousy, for they didn't have the money the stewards had, what with all the tips we got.

The officers were over the greasers and trimmers in the engine room, which, by the way, was the cleanest part of the ship where everything was polished. The steel steps, handrails and decks were always gleaming and all the brass clocks and pressure gauges shone like the fender and brass strip across the mantel my mother thought so much of at home. It's true the old saying, 'When shite gets up it's hard to put down', for these officers would try to pull rank and, generally speaking, weren't liked amongst the catering staff. As for me, well, I was lucky, for you would have to tell me you were going to hurt me physically or verbally before I would react. I enjoyed life and nothing bothered me. To get back to my story: their food was cooked in the main kitchen, so it was my job to go down from the mess in the sundeck by private elevator to the kitchen and pick up all their food in large dixies, which were then transferred into hot presses and *bains-marie*, in the engineers' pantry, and it was from there I served it out. By doing this I got a good grounding in the run of the kitchen: how the food was cooked, what was served with what – the whole history – and it was in a much more relaxed atmosphere. All this happened before the kitchen would be overrun with screaming waiters.

I spent five round trips with the *Queen* and during this time a dreamboat was launched, the latest in cruising. She was the only one built specially for pleasure and she was named RMS *Caronia*, or the 'green goddess', for her superstructure was painted two shades of green. What with her red, white and black funnels, she was a real picture at 34,000 tons, with the lines of a yacht – the smallest ship I'd been on to date. She did her maiden cruise around the continent of Africa, down the west coast, up along the east, through the Red Sea and Suez and back home through the Mediterranean to New York. She was known as a dollar-earner for England, since all her passengers were Yanks, and for a long period after the war the dollar bill became the flag of all nations.

The cruise lasted about sixteen weeks and as waiters we were assigned the same people throughout the voyage. You win some, you lose some. I had a guy in another cruise jumped overboard about two days out from Capetown and when they threw him a lifebelt he just swam away from it. Let's get back to the *Caronia*, even if your man didn't! Her next big cruise was '50 into '51 around the world. It was to be an epic cruise, and so it was, though not in the way that was planned. The crew complement was 650 and the passenger complement should have been the same but just before the ship sailed there was a spate of cancellations. We sailed with 112 passengers, 35 entertainment staff classed as passengers and 600 crew. The cancellations had come about because the Korean War was in full swing. The Americans didn't think it proper to be seen traipsing around the world enjoying themselves whilst their sons and daughters were being slaughtered in Korea.

I'm sure the company lost money but the publicity was fantastic, for in Long Beach, California, the port for Los Angeles, we served 1,100 people dinner and most of these were guests of the passengers, while a lot of stars came down from

Hollywood. A very conservative figure on the cost of that one meal back in 1951 would be 10 dollars a head, amounting to 11,000 dollars and that was food alone, never mind the drinks. We had a history of serving free meals around the world. If you were a passenger and called into some place where you had friends, chances were you invited them on board for dinner on the house, or in this case on the 'ship'. I served cab-drivers and all sorts that passengers met ashore and invited back on board for dinner. It was ludicrous, I know, but sure I was only the waiter. One fellow in particular was a grand master or had some title like that in a Freemason lodge somewhere in the midwest of the States, and every port we called at he had a whole bunch of these guys in for dinner or lunch. A few of us waiters pooled our experiences with this guy and we worked out how much it cost the company to carry him. A low estimate of up to 1,000 guests at 10 dollars a head was arrived at and to crown it out he had one of the cheapest cabins possible (3,000 dollars) and to top that off even more, he never, never, tipped his waiter.

It was here in Long Beach I saw my first real live movie star, Van Johnson, but the night was too hectic, with me so busy serving caviare and filet mignon that I didn't even ask for his autograph. There were lots of other stars there too but Johnson was the flavour of the month. It was a brilliant cruise, a complete circuit of the world: west through the Panama into the South Seas to Japan, New Zealand, Australia, Malaya, Sri Lanka (or Ceylon, as it was then), India, Africa, the Mediterranean and home. God it was fantastic!

By now I had a brave understanding of the job and I could discuss the menu when asked. This was very important, for, as I said, the menu was partly in French and even the customer sometimes found it hard to comprehend. I must say that I got on like a house on fire and I really loved my job, for I treated every meal like opening night, with the dining-room the stage, breakfast, lunch and dinner the performances and me in the 'lead'. Cruising had a different atmosphere from the ordinary passenger service, for the client was more relaxed and, into the bargain, had more money to spend. To say they were wealthy would be an understatement, for it isn't everyone who can leave his home and business for six months in the year. I would say you would have had to be one of two things: well-off, or in retirement and well-off, but either way being well-off was the key. We had a Twenty Club on board and you had to have 20 million dollars to get in. This, by the way, wasn't open to the crew – I wonder why?

A lot of the passengers came back several times and I myself had two different couples do the world cruise with me in 1950–1951. They left the ship at Cherbourg, where we picked them up again the following year on the great Africa/India cruise and they hadn't been home in all that time. That's what I call living! The mistake was that most of us involved tried to live like the people we were serving. As I said, the cruising passengers were different because they wanted conversation and I loved chatting. The 'awfully' English passenger was more stand-offish and the waiter had to keep a discreet distance from the table and at the same time anticipate any of the customers' needs: making sure the condiments and such were close at hand, water glass filled two inches from the top, the proper wine glass filled, and above all, silence until you are spoken to first. I think this must have dated back to the days of Raj. It was a pleasure to go cruising, plus I got seeing a bit of the world, so I'll come back to those days later.

During this time I was going steady, if you could call it that, with Agnes and although we were many times a whole world apart, we kept in touch by letter through every port. Before sailing, the crew was issued with an itinerary and a list of agents around the world who catered for our mail, so I would leave copies with my mother and with Agnes. I really looked forward to mail call as soon as we hit the beach. We wrote nearly every day to each other and as time went on and we married I continued going to sea as it was expected, for you see that was my job and I thought I could do nothing else.

REMEMBER PEARL HARBOR

Cruising was a great time in my life, for here I was a young lad with no real education and getting a chance to see the world in luxury. Nowadays it's old hat to go here and there, but up to thirty years ago, before the planes took over the travel business, it took time to go from one place to another. Overseas vacationing was for them 'what could afford it'. When I joined the *Caronia* in Southampton in 1950 it was October and I was twenty years of age. We set sail for New York via the Bahamas carrying the remnants of the old Empire stock going to winter there. That part of the trip was very sedate and the dining-room wasn't too crowded. The waiter, however, had to be on his toes and do a wee bit of bowing and scraping, for this was the old aristocracy and made you feel like a lackey. The Yanks were absolutely different, more relaxed and friendly. It took us five days to Hamilton, Bermuda, where we stayed overnight and apart from the language difference it was much the same as the Canaries. I wasn't really impressed.

Maybe I was looking forward to New York again, for two days later we arrived in the Hudson with your woman still standing with her right arm stretched up holding the torch. She was on our port, or left-hand side, with the Battery on our starboard, or right-hand side. The river was as busy as I had left it a couple of months before, with cargo barges being pushed about by the little bullies of tugs, honking their way through the crowds of similar floating vessels. I could spend ages watching the antics of this traffic and the only other comparable place was Hong Kong. There must have been traffic regulations working somewhere otherwise things would really have got jammed up. After the pilot had come on board at the Battery, the tugs would gather alongside like weans round their mother's skirt and tie on. They would then nudge her gently into her berth, which was at right angles to the run of the river. The passengers would have to assemble in the designated lounges for immigration and customs clearance, for there was no such thing as sending up your maid or manservant here. Meanwhile the waiters were detailed to take the hand luggage ashore and stand under the first letter of the owner's surname until the passenger came and collected all his luggage. Only then would a customs official mark it for clearance.

It sounds laborious but within an hour after docking the passengers would have disembarked and the ship would be in the process of getting cleaned up, stored up and making ready

136

for sailing day again, usually in thirty-six hours. Everything would be relaxed again as soon as the passengers went ashore and the stewards, of which I was one, could go through the passengers' quarters in jeans and singlets while working or scrubbing floors on our knees. It wasn't all sunshine, I can tell you, but about 1 pm all work stopped for the day, so there was nothing to do but get dressed and go up town. The best thing about a big ship was that you had so many people to choose from when making friends, and you could meet so many different kinds at sea at this time. The war wasn't long over and I met many strange fellows; between guys that were shell-shocked and fellows of a theatrical nature it was a bit of a culture shock. Thank God I got by.

Speaking of the war, a lot of fellows had wartime commissions and now all of a sudden the war was over and these lads found themselves out in civvy street with no stripes. For that reason the 'big ships' seemed to be a great attraction for them. To give you an example of how bad it was: we had a plate house, where, as in my first job, dishes were washed, and there were nine fellows working in it. The lowest rank employed there was a flight lieutenant while the others were squadron leaders, wing commanders and such – that's how it was. The sea at that time attracted these young men spoiled by five years of being pampered and with wartime commissions, giving orders. They were too young before the war and there was no place for them after it. Their country needed them at the time and then having used them dropped them. I remember one guy, an ex-Spitfire pilot who used to eat aspirins by the score and lie in his bunk in a daze. We also had our share of amputees, lacking an arm or leg, who did specialised jobs as lift attendants and such.

It was good, too, listening to some of the stories of the war. Don't forget that it was only five years before that the world ceased to be in turmoil, so it was still fresh in their minds. Some of the most horrific stories came from men in the Royal Navy who ran the Russian convoys. They were attacked both by torpedoes and bombs, often having to jump overboard into the water with the ship's oil ablaze round them. The survival time in the water was a matter of minutes; otherwise they froze to death. I loved listening to some of the older men; come to think of it, they were all older. I can remember a fellow telling me about the sinking of the *Empress of Britain* and the acts of bravery he saw that day as she was sinking. I thought to myself, what a small world, too, for, as I told you, I recalled looking at a hatch cover with the *Empress of Britain* stamped on it that was washed on the beach at the Isle of Doagh. What a story that hatch cover could have told but instead it was used as a barn door for years. Who knows? it may still be there. Another fellow I sailed with claimed to have been Monty's batman and he talked about El Alamein. You know, if I'd written it all down I could have been a Second World War historian.

One of the cruises I did was to Japan and it was really a tour of the American theatre of war in the Pacific. It was a memorable cruise for we sailed with 600 crew and 400 passengers from New York, all Yanks. Since we were still dollar-earners there were no English passengers on board. Britain may have won the war but she was still on her knees. Rationing of commodities did not finally cease till 1954 but that was their problem, for we were away to the South Pacific. It was early January in New York – the coldest place in the world in winter, I always thought. We sailed at sundown and awoke next morning to brilliant sunshine as we ran along the coast of Florida, making our way to Curaçao in the Dutch West Indies where we loaded up with oil for the trip. It seems it paid the master to do this. It was also worth the visit to the quaint little Dutch settlement there in Willemstad where the people acted as in old Amsterdam in traditional Dutch dress.

It must have been exciting to go exploring all those years ago, settling people in different parts of the unknown world and claiming them as your own. Here was a wee place 5,000 or 6,000 miles away from Holland being owned and ruled by people who have maybe never even seen it. We sailed from there to Caracas in Venezuela. Now actually, to get to Caracas by sea you have to sail into La Guaira and either go through a tunnel in the mountain or go over it by car. I can tell you the latter way was hair-raising to say the least, as one side of the road just dropped away hundreds of feet and the drivers, knowing they were putting the wind up you, enjoyed it. At the top of this hill looking down into Caracas was like looking into Aladdin's cave with all the bright lights. (I often get reminders of that sight, though in a smaller scale, if I drive into town over Piggery Ridge. From there you have a panoramic view of Derry, Waterside and the Foyle estuary with its two bridges, and away in the distance the seaside lights of Moville on the Inishowen side and the security lights of Magilligan prison on the Derry side.) By the way, La Guaira at the time of my visit was the busiest airport in the world. I saw that for myself: as one plane was taking off another was touching down. This traffic was between North and South America though I'm sure other airports have equalled it now.

Looking down into Caracas reminded me of one other place which had a similar problem. That was away in New Zealand on the other side of the world where we took in Christchurch on the Canterbury Plains. To get there we had to dock in Lyttelton and either go through the tunnel or over the mountain to Christchurch. This trip in contrast with that to Caracas was more relaxing, and coming off the top of the hill into Christchurch was like a scene from Walt Disney's *Peter Pan*. I'm digressing again.

We left Caracas and sailed west to Maracaibo and on then to

Cartagena, where all the pirates whom we played at a few years before had made their haven. There were still old ruins of forts and castles and a lot of pirate lore about the place and, as the tourists hadn't yet started to come in their droves, it was still as 'olde world' as it was all those years ago. Untouched. I was in another world. Out of Cartagena, west to Panama and here I pictured Red Beard and his horde crossing the isthmus, sacking the town of Panama and stopping short. If he'd gone a wee bit further north he would have hit Hollywood and maybe got in the movies there. But let me go back a bit, if I may, before Panama.

We entered the Panama Canal at Colón on the Caribbean side. I make that point because the canal runs north–south and not east–west. Here the captain handed over control to an American pilot and crew, who took the ship through the lakes and locks. The locks acted in a similar way as in the canals running through England, only on a much larger scale. That trip we were the largest vessel to pass through them and at 35,000 tons it was a pretty tight squeeze. As we progressed through, one of the cruise staff – something like a courier nowadays – gave the passengers and crew a talk on the canal itself: whose brainchild it was, when it was built and by whom, how many lives were lost on construction and who controlled it now. It was much more interesting than the Suez Canal, as there seemed many more things to do in such a short passage.

As I said, an American crew took charge and we were just pulled along by 'mules', small trains on tracks on either side of the locks. It was a great operation, typical Yankee, and years later when I went to live in California, I drove along the same road and crossed the bridge which had lifted, when we went through one of the locks, with all the traffic on both sides waiting to pass. The name of that highway is the Pacific Coast Highway 101 and it runs from Nome, Alaska, to Lima, Peru.

At the time of our crossing it was classed the longest highway in the world. We passed through, I think, three locks and two manmade lakes (or was it the other way about?). Anyway, we got to Panama on the Pacific side.

I was getting used to these places now, Spanish or Portuguese being the spoken language, and the buildings similar to Cádiz or Barcelona. We sailed out into the Pacific and I should mention that the weather was glorious and the passengers content. I say this, for when a number of people are together in close company there is bound to be discontent, even with people that rich. Money isn't everything; it's only something to go a message with! With the ship set on course for Hawaii, five days away, we stewards could relax to serving three meals a day, and settle down to a steady routine. However, as stewards we were also in the front line as ambassadors for the Cunard White Star Company. There was always a certain air of decorum. As soon as the ship hit the tropics a gang of us would sleep out at night on deck, although in port we slept in our cabins because the gnats or mosquitoes would bite the arse off you. It was sheer delight to wake up in the morning and hear birds, yes birds! chirping and fighting to get a place to land on board. We were island-hopping our way across the Pacific and even if we couldn't see land, you can rest assured that it was just over the horizon, consequently the birds. They love to follow ships.

The porpoise was another great favourite, and it was fascinating to watch them run alongside and scratch themselves on the fo'c's'le, or in landlubber's language, the sharp end. We would pass shoals of them like a long monster bobbing up and down in the water. One morning we were awakened by the loud deep sound of the ship's horn and as the ship took a sharp tilt we all rushed to the side to see what was happening. The horn blasted off again and then for a third time. Since it was 6 am, there were one or two sore heads but they soon cooled off when they found out that we were passing the Island of Molokai, where Father Damien, the Belgian priest, had set up his leper colony and died there of leprosy himself. Now we were paying tribute to him. I thought this was a lovely gesture. As the deck officers of the watch assembled at the after end, the red duster was raised and then lowered to half-mast. The engines stopped and there was a minute's silence. Then the horn blasted three times again, and with engines ticking over and the morning sun pushing the night out of its way we sailed on into the horizon, the silence only broken by the seagulls squawking. We all stood there deeply moved, passengers and crew alike. Maybe I'm an old softie but there was a hint of 'mist' in the eye.

From Molokai we sailed into a lovely wee cove called Hilo, another of the Hawaiian group and there the canoes came out to meet us, even though it was 6 am. We dropped anchor and lowered our own lifeboats which we used as ferries because it wasn't every place we could tie up. We used our lifeboats as 'buses' to and from the ship. It used to be fun getting the elderly – and they were all elderly – off the ship into the ferry and then getting them ashore off the ferry. That's where we came in, for we had to double up our jobs. The Hawaiian music was in the air and the hula girls, dressed in their grass skirts, came on board to dance for the passengers; everything was for the passengers but I suppose it was only right since they were paying for it. It wasn't like me to miss a good thing, so I was there in the middle. The custom was to place a garland, or lei, of very sweet-smelling flowers around your neck and rub noses. When sailing away from the island you cast the lei back in the waters and if it floated back to shore you would return. Mine did but I never got back to Hilo – yet!

We spent the daylight hours at Hilo and with the sun going down on the horizon – where else? you might ask – we sailed for Honolulu, arriving next morning at six, where the same performance happened, the only difference being that these girls were more professional. I think they worked for the tourist board. I got plenty of photos of them dancing the hula. I suppose it was the haymaker's jig, Hawaiian style. Hawaii, although not a state at the time, was very American and being an army and navy base naturally was full of American soldiers and sailors. Every other shopfront was a saloon. We had tours laid on for the passengers and the crew. There was one up to a living volcano, Mauna Loa, and another round to Pearl Harbor where the Japanese sank the most of the Pacific fleet on the morning of 7 December 1941, only nine short years before. The hulks were still there and we got the whole story from a Japanese tourist guide who was almost crying telling us. I was searching into his face and eyes to see if he was really crying.

The first time I heard the slogan 'Remember Pearl Harbor!' was from an American soldier being thrown out of Willy Campbell's pub in Duke Street and now here was I being shown all round it and the evidence was still there. We also visited Soldiers' Field where later the classic film *From Here To Eternity* was filmed.

Pineapples are to Hawaii what the spuds are to Ireland and they are to be seen everywhere you go. This was long before the man from Del Monte came! We had a conducted tour around a pineapple farm, picked our pineapples, brought them to the cannery and watched them being processed and canned with our names on the tin. After three days in Honolulu it was time to move on west.

A day at sea to rest up and get a wee bit of order into our lives again, for the shore parties and tours can take it out of you, especially if you are over sixty-five or seventy, and then on to Midway. This island, much like the rest, came into the public notice on account of the war, for it was here that the Yanks sank most of the Japanese taskforce and turned the tide of the war in the Pacific. I think James A. Michener may have used this battle in his *Tales of the South Pacific*, from which the musical and the very successful movie *South Pacific* was taken. After a day sailing round Midway we steered west to Wake Island, and crossed the international date line, where everybody gets themselves into a tizzy about what day it is. Depending which way you are travelling, you either lose a day or gain a day and on this particular trip we crossed it a couple of times. That meant that one week we had a couple of Thursdays and no Tuesdays, or something like that. One thing I *am* sure of: I missed my twenty-first birthday on that cruise, for I went to bed on Tuesday night and next day was Thursday. Wednesday, my birthday, hadn't showed up.

We arrived at Wake, where as usual we had to anchor out in the bay and use our lifeboats, and, believe it or not, there was still war debris on the beach: landing craft, remnants of tanks, both American and Japanese, pieces of artillery and lots of rusted coiled barbed wire lying about. I felt I had been there before, as it was only a few short years since I was sitting in the Midland picture house glued to my seat trying to warn Robert Taylor – the last marine left – that the sneaky Japs had him surrounded. As far as I remember, he 'bought it' as the Limeys would say. Looking at this wee island now, I wondered what it was all about; was it worth the loss of all those lives?

SOME ENCHANTED
EVENINGS

From Wake we went to Guam in the Marianas, where there was still a large American presence and I guess there must have been fighting there too, for the landing beaches still had weapons of war strewn about the place.

I would like to tell you a wee story on that subject. When we got to Yokohama, which is the port for Tokyo, our master had a guest – another captain but in the Royal Navy – it seems they were at sea school as boy cadets. Anyway, the skipper was entertaining him and I was serving them at table. Can you picture me standing at a discreet distance from the table, with my waiter's cloth over my arm, when the captain made a remark to his guest about 'our boxing waiter' and I was introduced? Seems unlikely but that's exactly what happened. The guest asked what part of Ireland I came from and I told him the North, Derry, to which he replied, 'Aha! Londonderry.' I said, 'At home we call it Derry.' So having got that out of the way, he told me he was commander of the barracks then called Sea Eagle and that his butcher supplier in Derry was May Quigley from Duke Street and that he used to get a few sides of beef and fly them over to London for parties. I said, 'That's strange, for it took my mother all her time to get her ration of sausages or mince off her.' It just goes to show that 'murder will out' and I had to go all the way to Japan to find out that our family butcher was dealing in the black market. It really is a small world. He was quite a nice fellow and when the conversation lulled I stepped back again from the table; that's how it was.

His job was scrap merchant for the Admiralty and he was in charge of all the debris on the beaches and the sunken ships, of which there were plenty. I'll never forget Manila, for there were so many Japanese ships sunk, I'm told all in the one day, that they just pulled them to one side to make a channel into the docks. It seems that a combined taskforce of Yanks and Australians caught the Japanese cargo fleet on the hop. I witnessed this also in Victoria in the Seychelles but this time they were warships. I remember standing on deck that morning counting thirty or more hulks lying on their sides or standing nose or arse up out of the water. It really was a sight to see and I wondered what state the crews were in during the blitz. As John Wayne or Robert Mitchum might have said, it must have been hell there.

Yokohama was really different from any place we had been

to before. It was cherry-blossom time and the streets were lined with cherry trees. They were even growing in the shops. The people were most courteous and when you went into a shop the assistants were all over you to make a sale. The merchandise was all new to us; toys both mechanical and electrical were a big hit because England was still in the grip of 'austerity'. I bought six china teasets, which was odd since they were really made in Japan. We still have two of those sets at home and I bought them over forty years ago. From Yokohama we sailed round to Nagasaki, where the second atomic bomb 'to end the war' was dropped on 9 August 1945. Although they had started to rebuild, the place was in a shambles. It still seems to me that it was a crime against humanity and no excuse could be accepted. (President Harry Truman could say whatever he liked. I think he was just flexing his muscles and all those people died.)

Next day we were in Kobe, similar to Yokohama but here we were treated to an opera. *Madame Butterfly*, what else? After a couple of days in Kobe we set sail for Okinawa and here we visited the Teahouse of the August Moon. I think somebody wrote about it and it was later made into a play and film. Fighting took place here too and there were a lot of graves. The corpses, I've been told, were brought home to military cemeteries in the USA. From Okinawa to Manila, passing between the two sentries Bataan and Corregidor at the mouth of the bay of Manila. Bataan was featured in one of the American war movies. I think the great Wallace Beery was a marine in it. As a kid I loved that sort of stuff, as it was more interesting than the British fighting. Maybe it was the background of sand and palm trees and Japs doing dirty tricks on the good guy or was it the slang the Yanks used? Whatever, the sets were more interesting.

Corregidor was where General MacArthur left the Philippines in a big hurry, calling back over his shoulder, 'I shall . . . '

or was it 'I *will* return'? Anyway, he got away himself and left his men to fend for themselves. It took him about three or four years to get back and there's a big deal of publicity about him wading in from a landing-craft saying, 'I have returned.' Maybe he didn't say those words at all. With him wading through water it was more probably, 'Jeeze, this water's wet.'

We dropped the flag once again – it was getting to be a habit – to half-mast in respect to the fallen dead and also to those who died in the prison-camps. I'm told the Japanese weren't the nicest jailors.

I met Father Joe Shields, a school pal of mine, in Manila. We shared the same desk together in the Waterside Boys' School in between going to the Christian Brothers' and the tech. I hadn't seen Joe since leaving school six or seven years before, so it was a real treat for both of us, as this was Joe's first month in the Philippines. He took me out to his mission hut outside the town, and on the way we passed another priest dressed in long white robes sitting on a ribshaker of a horse. We stopped and your man threw his leg over the horse's neck and was introduced to me as Father O'Donnell from Donegal. He took his bag from the horse, called some wee lad, left him the horse and rode home with us in the car. There were about eight other priests at the house, in what seemed to me to be the middle of the jungle. Next day was a Friday and we all went to a resort up in the hills overlooking a dead volcano and I found out that it was only the Irish that kept days of abstinence, for when it came to order lunch, I was the only one to have fish and the priests made fun of me.

That was forty-four years ago and a priest came to Derry last year to promote the missions. He stayed in the Nazareth House near my home and while out for a walk one afternoon I met him. He stopped to pass the time of day. I half-recognised his face and after asking him a couple of questions, I told Father

O'Donnell I had met him in Manila over forty years ago and to prove it I had a picture of him, Joe Shields and myself up in my house. Nothing would do him but he would come up to the house where I produced the photo and he was over the moon. I'm told he retold this story in his talks later. You might wonder what he was doing with the horse in the first place, well he was coming back from a retreat. This is where the priest goes to the villages and catches up on baptisms, marriages and funerals. Some of these people may not see a priest for a year or more and it's not unusual for a man and woman to turn up at the church to get married and them with two or three weans.

Port Moresby on Papua New Guinea was another good stop and although it was for only a day, it turned out very exciting, as the local tourist board rounded up 2,000 or more natives of all ages to give us an exhibition of their dancing. The ones to pay attention to were the big fellows wearing the bird-of-paradise headdress, for one of the criteria for wearing this was that you had to have performed an act of cannibalism. Take it from me there were plenty of them around with the headgear. One of the Australian administrators told me that there were still Japanese in the jungle who did not know the war was over. The natives didn't care, for I'm sure they ate away at them. I should mention here that the girls wore only skirts but funny thing about it, nobody took any notice after the initial shock. These natives were all gathered in a large field – like the Kilfennan sports – and were broken up into different age groups doing various dances. It all looked the same to me but then all Irish dancing and music, I think, looks and sounds the same.

After being told about the cannibals I was a bit wary about moving around on my own. I was aware that some of the natives kept pointing me out to one another and it seems my red hair was the attraction. I noticed that a lot of the men dyed their hair with betel nut and chewed it as well which left their mouths all red. I got a bit of a gunk, though, when I made my way through a crowd of sweaty bodies and in the centre of this mass of flesh I found a native, with the cannibal headgear on, sitting against a tree, playing a guitar and singing in the best American drawl you ever heard, 'Away up in the mountains so happy and free/I wish I was back on my own mother's knee . . .' Maybe he ate Johnny Cash! It was then that I came to the conclusion that it might be a bit of a 'put on' for the passengers.

We now started our homeward journey, sailing southeast to Nouméa, New Caledonia. This French island is rich in manganese ore used in the steel industry but it became uneconomical to ship it back to France. After the war the mining stopped and the place became derelict and looked forgotten. It's like a dream to me that I visited a penal colony there and it looked like another I had seen on Devil's Island in French Guiana, on the northeast coast of South America. This is the infamous prison that featured in many books and films. All I can say is the French knew how to incarcerate people. The others were only playing at it.

Everybody that could sail a boat in days gone by must have headed out to the Pacific to grab themselves an island, for the French, Americans, British and Portuguese are all represented there. We made our way round these lovely islands and the shorelines were just as inviting as you would dream about or see in a glossy magazine. We often came in as close as we could and watched the natives fishing. Oh, what an idyllic life it looked!

After a day in Suva, capital of Fiji, off we went to Tonga, where we were greeted by Queen Salote, or Queen Nuku'alofa, as she was known locally. She was the girl that stole the show at Elizabeth II's coronation when she rode to the ceremony in an open-topped carriage in the rain. Though she weighed about twenty stone, she was an instant success and the English people took her to their hearts. We saw her a few years before that, of course, and she was an instant success with us too, for she threw a beach-party, a luau – where else but on the beach – and whilst it was billed for the passengers, we, the crew, were not turned away. It was a night to remember, for we had roast sucking pig, local fresh fish wrapped in leaves and baked, barbecued birds, possibly some of the seagulls that followed us about from island to island. It doesn't matter now, for they tasted fabulous. Then there were men dancing on hot coals and with the local hooch in abundance some of the crew had to be restrained from emulating them. A great night was had by all.

From Tonga we sailed east to Pago Pago, pronounced with an 'n', 'Pango Pango'. This island got its notoriety from the fact that Somerset Maugham set his famous short story 'Rain' there. Based on fact, it tells of the relationship between Sadie Thompson, an American prostitute, and a clergyman. They made a movie about it in 1953 called *Miss Sadie Thompson* and the star role went to Rita Hayworth. We sailed on south-southeast, to the island you always mention when talking about the South Seas, Tahiti, in French Polynesia. This island really stood out and we lay outside the reefs, as usual using our lifeboats as ferries. The water was crystal clear and the sea life made it a diver's paradise. With the bumboats around us like seaweed, the noise and banter were terrific and as in most of the other islands they did a good line in primitive carvings of sailfish, coconut straw mattings and baskets. I could have stayed in Tahiti with very little coaxing but strangers are taboo and not allowed residence.

After a day in Tahiti we moved east again to Pitcairn, one of the two loneliest islands in the world. The other island being Tristan da Cunha in the South Atlantic, which, in my opinion, is the loneliest of the two. It can be very cold and stormy. The island is used by whaling fleets and the islanders speak English with a Cornish accent, left over from shipwrecked English sailors who later colonised the place. From what I could see they were sitting at the bottom of a volcano, which, I must tell you, exploded a few short years after we first visited and destroyed the island. There was a big emergency airlift to get them to safety and most of them came to Southampton. Missing the way of life, they decided to go back and pick up the pieces. I haven't heard hilt nor hair of them since.

I wasn't allowed ashore on Pitcairn because I was a Catholic. I thought I had left all that behind in 'Londonderry' but it looks like some Ulsterman got out there first. The truth of the story is that after the *Bounty* ran up on the beach, the only thing that Fletcher Christian took off her was the Bible and from that they all stuck to one religion, Seventh Day Adventist. Glad to say, we Catholics weren't alone because communists were also barred.

Most of the islanders came on board and the doctor gave a lot of them medical checks. As the American dentist looked at their teeth, he was heard to remark that he had never seen such healthy teeth. He took a lot of pictures and notes to take back to his alma mater or someplace. I said most of the islanders came on board but at least two were missing, for there was a fellow in jail for stealing and neither him nor the jailor could come off the island, so they both waved from the small pier. We all waved back, not at all concerned that the guy was a con.

Leaving Pitcairn was very touching, for the sun was going down and the islanders gathered around us in their boats – they live off the sea – and as the engines started to turn slowly, the *Caronia* shuddered slightly, as if out of a sleep and as the swell rose the wee boats took on a very lonely look bobbing in concert with the seagulls. The people started singing in unison 'We Shall Gather By The River' and we slowly made our way out towards the horizon. There was a long silence and everybody on deck just drifted away to their stations and left the deckhands to stow the ropes and such away. I'll always remember it.

There was another instance similar to that, in Madras, where a platoon of Indian soldiers came down to the pier; it was one of the few places where we could go alongside the wharf and tie up. The soldiers drilled, played music and marched up and down the docks all day, and they were made up of a couple of bands, bagpipe, brass and trumpet. They really did a good job in all the heat, but sundown came – the time for sailing – and the band started playing 'Will Ye No' Come Back Again?' and 'Auld Lang Syne', and I can tell you it was a real tearjerker. At all the New Year's Eve parties I've been to, before or since, 'Auld Lang Syne' never sounded the same and my mind ever wanders to that day leaving Madras.

I enjoyed the Pacific but I should say I saw it at its best. There were no high-rise hotels or flats or beaches spoiled with commercialism, and just to see it like we saw it, from the lagoons and breakwaters or reefs, was magic. I just hope but doubt that it's still unspoiled.

THAT SOUTH
AMERICAN WAY

On we sailed, going easy to Honolulu, and a strange thing – I was going to say 'funny' but it was too serious – happened. The night before we docked in Honolulu a list was posted on our noticeboard and myself and at least thirty others were ordered to report at the storage hatch, where we were detailed off to transport all the fresh fruit and vegetables, spuds, the lot, up to the stern and dump them over. Hawaii came under the US import regulations and one of them was a ban on importing fresh foods. We spent three hours at this and next morning when we docked beside the Big Pineapple, there was a restock of the stuff we dumped the previous night. Don't forget we had about a thousand people on board to feed and the nearest port now was Los Angeles, five days away.

We spent a couple of days again in Honolulu and then on to Los Angeles. I'd been there a year before and I looked up some Derry people I knew from school, the Kyle family. There were no stars on board as on my earlier round the world cruise but I got a chance to go up into Hollywood to see the stars' homes. It was a great chance for a wee boy from Fountain Hill but then I was easy pleased. We left Los Angeles for New York, calling at Acapulco, Mexico, on the way. I'm sure that Acapulco is a lot different now from what it was in 1950 when it was a millionaire's playground. We arrived in a beautiful natural basin and anchored right in the middle of things. No tugboats or barges here, just a playpool for water-skiing and lazing around in fabulous launches with a bevy of bathing beauties on every one of them. Mind you, they got some whistles from us. It was about 6.30 am and a fleet of fishing launches cruised in with their catch trailing behind them: sailfish about six to eight feet long, turtles about three feet across the shell, and marlin about six feet long.

I was interested in the marlin since a reporter in Auckland gave me a write-up in the local sportspaper before a fight there. He started off the piece with, 'Although this lad is no bigger than a marlin spike, he feels cramped in anything under 30,000 tons', and then went on to print verbatim everything I had said. He had been asking me questions and since I couldn't see him write anything down I talked away and I told him about the conditions on board, all about my job. Then he took my picture so I could not deny it when the story was printed. It gave the impression that the cruise was for the crew's benefit, so the chief steward sent for me and showed me the newspaper and, as we say in Derry, 'he was brave and mad at me'. I was more interested in my picture and what they said about me to be too worried about him and, anyway, he was always half-cut and forgot about it next day. I don't mean to be too unkind but when someone poured him a drink it had to go in to a tall glass, half-full, so that he wouldn't spill it in his lap, for he had a severe dose of the shakes. I'm sure he was a good candidate for gout.

In Acapulco I nipped in and got my picture taken with some fellow's catch on the jetty. It looked authentic enough and I still have it, and depending on who I'm showing it to, it's *my* catch or not. Who's to know anyway?

Acapulco has the most perfect setting I've ever seen. We visited a hotel on the side of the cliff and watched an exhibition of high-diving from the cliffs, which took place a couple of times a day. In the evening when the divers carried fire torches for effect, what with the danger, it was really spectacular. The place was packed with Americans down from California and Texas for weekends, at 10,000 dollars a time, which was money back in 1950.

The world really is ill-divided: here we were in all this luxury, pandering to every whim and wish of all these old relics with one foot in the grave and aware of the poverty that we witnessed around us. It wasn't called the Third World then but the poverty existed all the same. I saw people with no hope sitting along the streets in Madras just waiting to die. I'll never forget that and it couldn't be blamed on floods or natural disasters either.

We left Acapulco behind and headed down to Panama again, where we experienced the same things going through the canal and back to New York. Remember the exercise of dumping the fresh fruit and vegetables overboard before Honolulu? Well, we had a repeat performance the night before sailing into New

York. No wonder the company went broke, which I think it did. On that point the crew didn't help either, for the waste was out of this world. When joining a ship – I'm talking about the big ships not cargo boats – the first thing you get is your article number (same as a works number), then your lifeboat number, your emergency fire-drill number and last of all your cabin number. Now, from your mates, who most probably you have sailed with before in other ships, you'll get to know the 'perks' of the job, like getting food from the first-class menu: Chateaubriand, pheasant-under-glass on a bed of wild rice, roast rib of prime American beef (from the Kansas City market), full saddles or crowns of lamb, squab pigeon by the half-dozen (they were small!) duck à l'orange, and if you were fond of stews, there were all sorts of casseroles to choose from. There was caviare, grossly overrated, but I loved it. I ate it by the soup spoon on Melba toast, with hard boiled eggs and finely chopped onion. My favourite was pâté de foie gras – nothing more than the enlarged liver of a goose which had been force-fed – served with Melba toast; it was a food for the gods.

As we sailed around the world we would purchase the local produce, whether it be of the land or the sea. Lobster and crab were a great favourite of mine too. For soup we had a lobster bisque then broiled lobster, lobster thermidor or lobster Newburg. It was all good packing and it's surprising how you could acquire a taste for these fine foods. The crab was a bit more delicate and we even brought on live turtle for turtle soup. I can still see the turtles hanging up in the butcher's shop, with their throats slit being bled to death. Then we had our fill of oysters and clams. By the way, these all came on board alive. I know, for during the meal when passing through the pantries some smart aleck would scare the daylights out of you by shoving one of these wicked crabs or lobsters in your face. The ice cream we carried was really superb. It was American but I think

157

it must have been made specially for Cunard, for later when I went to live in Los Angeles, I searched for it in different super-markets. It was to no avail, for I never came across it again. It was called Dolly Madison. But the choicest ice-cream of all, though, was the cassata, which came on board at Naples and only lasted a couple of days, for the crew ate most of it.

I'm serious about this, and on reflection the cruises were run for the crew or so it seemed. There was an unbelievable amount of plunder – caviare, roasts of sirloin, legs of lamb, hams, chickens, eggs, butter – all seen as perks by the crew.

Disembarkation at New York was usually a bit quieter than sailing day, although there was still the hustle and bustle of longshoremen, the ever-present customs and immigration offi-cials, stewards running around with baggage, chauffeurs and taximen and relatives and maids waiting on their people, or 'pay check', coming home. I personally felt sad on these occasions because in the fifteen or sixteen weeks you had these people, you built up an attachment to them and they to you. If I'd taken up some of the many offers I got I'm sure someone else would have been writing this wee story, but life was too good and I wasn't up for adoption.

My trip around the South American continent was spec-tacular. We left New York and sailed south to the West Indies: Kingston, Port-au-Prince, to Curaçao for oil and on then to Caracas and Georgetown. From there on, life was idyllic as we sailed along the coast. We took it easy, for we had sixteen weeks to do it in, the weather was beautiful and we were going south with the sun. All meals except dinner were served on deck, though there were hot lunches available in the various saloons. The whole cruise had a carefree atmosphere about it but, as you know, when the graceful swan seems to glide effortlessly over the lake she's paddling away like hell underneath – well, that was us. Running along the coast at night, we could see a constant string of lights of seaports, the names of which we did not know. When I would be sitting on the aft rail, I used to wonder what sort of people they were, and did they know that a stranger like myself was thinking about them, sitting there watching them with the southern sky lit up by stars that were not to be seen in the northern sky. The Southern Cross is something to behold – and the electrical storms were marvellous too, for the sky would blaze as if someone turned on the light in a dark room. These storms would be a hundred or more miles away but the flash would seem overhead and lasted very long.

Our first big stop, Rio de Janeiro, was first seen by European eyes in January 1502, hence the name, and it is a truly beautiful harbour. There's no need to describe it, as I'm sure you've seen it so many times in travel brochures but I'd love to have been with those Portuguese explorers on that first day. It was breathtaking, to say the least, and the beach was fabulous. I think it is about fifteen miles long. Six or seven of us rented horses to go for a ride and away we went up the beach yipping and yoo-hooing. The horses battered on – come to think on it, so did we – and the first laugh was when one of the guys decided to ride through a large pool left by the tide on the beach and he finished up swimming, horse and all. The 'pool' was about twenty feet deep. Then the old horses reneged, so we all just got off, turned them loose and I never heard anything of them since. I'm sure they got home OK. They were probably used to doing that, anyway.

We took the usual ride by cable car to the top of Sugar Loaf and looked down on the splendour of Rio but there was squalor there too: behind Sugar Loaf was a shanty town were real poverty lurked, tin huts made from beaten-out tar barrels and open ditches carrying sewage. Overlooking all this is the famous statue of Christ the Redeemer on Corcovado and it seems the Argentines took it bad when the statue was built facing Brazil and its back to them. Lucky it wasn't the old Londonderry Corporation, for they would have had a statue of Carson or Craigavon looking down on the people of the Wells.

It seems the police are no better in Brazil than anywhere else. We were skylarking one evening coming back to the ship; there was no drink taken, so everybody had their senses about them when a couple of cops rounded us up. There were four of us, so they called the van, took us to the station, which was filthy, made us empty our pockets and put us into an even filthier pig-sty of a cell, and during all this time they wouldn't speak English. After separating us from our money and our papers and then keeping us for four or five hours, the pigsty door was opened and we were told to go. All our papers were on the table but the money had disappeared. In a situation like that you're as well to pick up your marbles, whatever's left of them, and bow out. I chalked it all up to experience.

Running south along the coast it took us ages to pass the lit-up skyline of São Paulo, Santos and a score of other smaller ports that seemed to run into one another. Finally we approached the entrance to the River Plate, where the scourge of the Atlantic convoys, the pocket battleship *Graf Spee*, became undone. For the short time she was out of Germany in action, she did a lot of damage to Allied shipping. The order went out to get her at all costs and after much searching the shipping lanes a couple of lesser ships, like terriers, spotted her and engaged her in bat-tle, slipped in under the dip of her guns and gave her such a going-over that her captain Hans Langsdorff had to pull into the River Plate and ask the Uruguayan government, which was neutral, for asylum or time to repair her damage. This sort of thing was acceptable in a neutral country. By international law she was allowed twenty-four hours for emergency repairs.

Well, the *Graf Spee* got seventy-two more hours to pull herself together, but it wasn't long enough, so she asked for more time but by then the *Ajax* and the *Achilles* had arrived and ringed the Plate off. The German ship had few options. You can imagine the hullaballoo back home in Germany, with the pride of the Third Reich contemplating surrender. Langsdorff took the only way out. He sailed his ship down the river just to within the three-mile limit and on 17 December 1939 scuttled her. When we arrived five years later she had been pulled out of the shipping lane but was still there as a kind of monument. As we passed her, both going up river and down, our ship dropped her flag to half-mast and sounded her horns in respect of a once great warrior of the sea. Again I thought it was a lovely gesture but then I'm a sucker for that sort of thing.

I was keeping myself in shape all this time by sparring on deck with the rest of the boys. By now we had a good number to choose from, enough to make up a boxing team, so we arranged a fight for our next port, Montevideo. On arrival we were taken up to an auditorium, where we weighed in and met our opponents. It seems to me that if you see one of these South Americans you've seen them all. There was no way I would ever have recognised my man again in a thousand years but I didn't care. He had two hands like me and that was all I needed. At the fight next evening the hall was packed with crew and passengers, all dressed up and smoking cigars. The second steward, my boss Jock McGowan, was the referee and as soon as my opponent climbed into the ring the ref came over to me to tell me in his best Glaswegian accent, 'This is not the guy you weighed in with; they've pulled a switch.' This took me back to Belfast, where I was billed to box one of the McCamberly brothers in a rematch. They were identical twins and I had boxed Fred and beat him but in the rematch two weeks later he sent his brother Jim to fight in his place, so I beat him too. Some fellow at the ringside caught it on and there was a whole investigation by the British Boxing Board. They both lost their licence for a period.

Well, back in Montevideo, where I was too cocky to be put off by a minor detail like that, I said, 'It doesn't matter. Let's get on with it', and we touched gloves and came out fighting. I somehow knew at once that I had the measure of him. I dropped him in the second round in his own corner and stood back for the count which seemed to take ages. It was as if the ref was coaxing him to get up and he was rising. He was on his feet and to my knowledge was ready for action but the ref seemed to be still counting, so there was nothing else for it but to take care of my own affairs. I hit the ref with the back of my right hand – more a good shove – then I rose off my feet into the air and into my opponent's chin with a left hook and down he went poleaxed with the crowd going wild.

The ring was encircled by a balcony and it was up there that all the locals gathered, though there were also some on my side of the ring on the groundfloor. Bottles and lit cigar butts and anything that was loose came pouring into the ring. At this point I was wishing I was back on my mother's knee again. I rushed out of the ring right into bother for the spectators started to kick me and punch me. Suddenly, into the crowd burst the chief butcher, a tank of a man all of twenty stone, and he calls, 'Follow me!' So I clung on behind him while he bulled his way through the crowd and got me out to safety and back to the ship.

You might wonder what happened to the ref. Well, before all hell let loose he was bowled across the ring and fell. He wasn't knocked out but he was annoyed at me and would have liked to say things to me. To be honest, the passengers said they never enjoyed a night like it, so your man thought it was great too – an ould lick. I got no money for the fight and I was the only winner that night. So much for Montevideo. I was glad to see the back of it. I went back two years later and since I had no fights lined up things were a bit quieter.

It was not unusual to 'lose' some passengers, as some would travel overland and join the ship again a couple of weeks later. For instance, I had passengers leave me in Rio and I didn't see them again till Valparaíso in Chile, though, needless to say, they paid as if they were still with you. It made life a lot easier, for instead of six people to 'nurse', you could finish up with two. One thing about the Americans, they expected to tip and the majority were generous, aye, some more than generous, but for tax reasons I must invoke the fifth amendment and say nothing.

We headed south to the Falklands and tied up in Stanley, a whaling station of yesteryear and now a sheep station. Most of the year it is cold and windy but this being January it was their summer.

We skirted the Antarctic Circle but the nearest we got to it was at Punta Arenas in Chile, the southernmost city in the world, which is about 900 miles from the South Pole. We didn't go round the Horn but instead slipped through the Strait of Magellan and found it more interesting, for we cruised past the last mountain in the backbone of the whole continent of America called Don Pedro Sarmiento Gumboa and it turned out to be a glacier with ice older than time, some say six miles deep and pure green in colour. It was sheer magic, with small icebergs floating all around us.

We moved on through the straits and early next morning we found ourselves in the South Pacific. On our way up the coast, sailing round different wee islands, we passed one called Londonderry Island. Nothing more than a whaling stop, but whaling was still a big business down there. I wondered what Derryman was that far south and named an island after his home town.

MIDNIGHT SUN

Valparaíso was the next stop. I think it was there I saw the guano birds, flying by the hundreds of thousands, and that's no exaggeration, over little islands and leaving their droppings, which over the years piled up to little hills of pure unadulterated bird shit. The locals set up a fertiliser business and exported guano all over the world. In the past twenty years or so the business went into decline, what with man overfishing the sardines that fed the birds and the use of artificial fertilisers. They have a big eco-problem there now. After a day in Valparaíso we went on up the coast to Callao, which is the port for Lima the capital of Peru. I had an address in my pocket that was given to me when leaving home of Alice Bryson, a neighbour/relation of my own, now Sister Anna. It was twenty-five years since she went out to Peru and, as I said before, there was no return for some missionary sisters or priests. I was detailed off to call on her.

The address was a bit vague but at the foot of the gangway I showed it to a customs official and his expression lightened. He said, all proud, 'Aah Seester Anna? Sure, I know her! She taught me. I show you.' He took me to a station and talked to some other fellow, and I was put on this train with open sides with the people getting off and on when they liked. It was magic: the dress, the shapes of the people and the baggage they had, which was anything from sheep, llamas – the first I ever saw – goats, tin buckets – the lot. It was all on this train winding its way up the side of a mountain with sheer drops below of hundreds of feet and no crash barriers. I have a bad head for heights – I'd fall off a sofa – so I had my gaze on the other side. It put me in mind of the ride in Venezuela from La Guaira into Caracas, spine-chilling to say the least.

It also brought to mind the trip I used to take to Dungloe in Donegal in the Lough Swilly bus, where it took four hours to travel a distance of about forty miles as the crow flies. The first twenty miles to Letterkenny was fine but after Letterkenny, the bus stopped at the foot of lanes, waiting on Annie or Cassie or Peter or John Johnny Willie, to appear. It was as if the bus driver knew they would come, for after waiting maybe ten or fifteen minutes someone would come down the lane. I can remember once a sheep being brought in, and there was also the odd bicycle in the back seat or up the middle of the isle. Those were great days altogether and I would say that those people in the bus didn't know or couldn't have cared less about the economic situation in eastern Tibet or Indo-China. They just got on with life, and so it was, here in Peru, at the other end of the world.

After travelling about four hours a fellow who had obviously been told to watch me took my arm and since he couldn't speak English I had to rely on hand signals or, as the tourist tends to do, speak louder. The train stopped and I got off. It seemed a million miles from nowhere but I couldn't say it was a one-horse town because all I could see was hitching posts and horses tied up to them just like in the old westerns; there were even the boardwalks and the dust road. In other words, it was like I had stepped into the screen of the Midland picture house in the middle of a cowboy picture.

I made a beeline to the best-looking building at the lower end of the town, rang the bell and a wee girl came out speaking either Spanish or Quechua. When I mentioned Sister Anna she flew away to get her. The funny thing is I had never laid eyes on Sister Anna before but I instantly knew who she was and there was a whole lot of running around introducing me here and there like a long-lost cousin. I was the first person to visit her since she had left Derry and we spent a lovely day, what was left of it, with me being bombarded with questions about home, all her family and the old neighbours, who, sad to say, were mostly gone to their rest. It was dark when she saw me to the train back to town and I felt very sad leaving her there away in the other end of the world but she put up a good front and smiled and asked me to pray for her. I often wonder did she cry after I left. I'm sure she did, for there was a tear in my eye. Again Pope John came up trumps, for Sister Anna came back to England some years ago and retired only in April 1994. She is eighty-five now and I would love to meet her again, someday.

Well, off we went out into the South Pacific to visit Easter Island and the island of Juan Fernández, better known as Robinson Crusoe Island, where Alexander Selkirk asked to be set ashore many years before, and – well, you know the story of Robinson Crusoe ... I had noticed a number of large logs about twenty feet long on the forward deck which had been brought aboard at Panama, and the ship's carpenter, Chippy, started to work on them. We the stewards weren't privy to what they were for but it turned out to be a raft he was making. One morning at sunrise, sleeping on deck, we were awakened by the silence of the engines. We looked over the side and there was our raft with one of the deck officers dressed up as Robinson Crusoe and steering the raft towards us was Man Friday, one of the crew blacked-up. It seems that during the night the raft was lowered away and towed to the island. This was Robinson Crusoe coming out to invite us onto his domain. Selkirk had had some sort of a row with his captain, William Dampier the privateer, and asked to be put off on Juan Fernández. He was there alone for five years until 1709. Defoe wrote *Robinson Crusoe* ten years later. We saw his cave and some of his cooking utensils and various traces of his being there. The passengers were agog, as was myself, for I too had read the story and loved it.

As for Easter Island, when we got there only one boat was lowered and a Mr Eaton, a very distinguished man, went ashore. He was a collector, so I guess he must have collected things on Easter Island. Several years later in Los Angeles I visited Forest Lawn cemetery where there are copies of three marvellous works of art of the life of Christ, namely, the Last Supper, the Crucifixion and the Resurrection, and Mr Eaton was one of the prime movers in putting them together. Special houses or auditoriums were built for this collection and it is worth a visit when in Los Angeles. There is also a small museum there, where some stones from Easter Island, with Eaton's name on them and the date of collection, and it was on that cruise that the finds were made. I stood looking that day at the pieces in the glass case and felt like saying to the rest of the visitors, 'I was there.' But like all these wee stories I kept it to myself till now.

It was only a couple of years before that that the Norwegian Thor Heyerdahl set out with a raft similar to the one we had to prove that Indians from South America were able to sail to Easter Island using the Humboldt Stream, something like our Atlantic Gulf Stream. He named his raft *Kon-Tiki* after the Inca sun god and I had the good fortune to see it in a museum in Oslo along with the *Fram*, the ship that took Amundsen down to the South Pole.

After Easter Island we headed east again to the Panama Canal and up the coast to New York. It was always great to get back to New York, for it was here you could catch up on the latest stage and film shows. I loved the excitement of Times Square, 42nd Street, Fifth Avenue and the subways. It was no bother walking the streets at night – certain streets, that is – for New York really didn't sleep. It was a tonic; I loved it. This was before the influx of Puerto Ricans who were American citizens. There was inevitably trouble between them and the Afro-Americans who were there before them.

The white gangs were just as bad, for I distinctly remember being caught in their crossfire one night just outside the dock gate and I finished up under a car which was part of a special cargo from England. There were about two dozen open-topped MGs just unloaded off the *Queen Elizabeth* and some of them got all shot up on the street while they were waiting for collection.

It was funny walking down 49th Street and seeing the people lying out at night on the fire escape to get a breath of air. This was before air-conditioning. The roofs were flat and this be-came a hazard because some kids around eighteen to twenty years of age – back home they would have been navvying or in the army but here they were 'kids' – would drop Coca Cola

168

bottles full of sand on you. You took your life in your hands when coming back on board at night. There's an age when this sort of thing doesn't bother you; now I'd think twice about going down the town here in Derry – at night, I mean.

The subways had become a hazard, too, before I left for good in 1961, for when going down to the station it was a relief to see other people there on the platform and in the train itself. You hoped that you wouldn't be the last one left, for gangs would roam through the train looking for single people or young couples and roll them for their money. It really wasn't very pleasant. My namesake, John Doran, whom I mentioned earlier, lived on Broadway. But sure Broadway is about twenty-five miles long and he lived in an apartment on the sixth floor on the borders of Harlem about ten or fifteen miles from Times Square. Eventually the Hispanics moved in there too and while waiting for the elevator in the apartment house you hoped that there was nobody in it when it came. Then when you got into the elevator and pressed your floor number, you hoped that it wouldn't go to the basement first, where a gang would be waiting to work you over. Don't think I am paranoid about this, for I witnessed it.

New York is still my dreamtown, though. I loved all the razzmatazz on the dock itself where we tied up. I was on kidding-and-talking terms with the longshoremen there and I was at an age when it was great to be popular. All the longshoremen called to me when I was going ashore and cracked jokes and pretended to spar with me. I loved that attention. The supervisor wanted me to come out to New York to live and box under his management. I just happened to be reading a story about him, how one of his boxers was in an insane asylum and he visited him regular every week bringing him lollipops. There was no way I was going to finish up like that. He wrote to my mother and explained how he was going to take care of me, for he would need her consent. His name was Nat Cohen and the guy he managed into the asylum was Ad Wolgast.

Time to sail again, this time to the Arctic Circle via Reykjavik, Iceland, then up to the North Cape, which is the most northerly part in Europe. It was here that we saw the midnight sun and I can tell you it was a sight to behold. When we pulled into this cove it looked disappointing; there was nothing there but sheer cliffs all around us and a wee hut at the end of a weather-beaten jetty. The hut turned out to be the post office. Don't ask me who manned it, or why, for when we took our letters in for posting the postmaster franked them and gave them back to us to post on board, just as in Guadalcanal. It was about 9 pm and we were detailed off to carry all the possible combinations of tea and coffee and milk in five-gallon thermos flasks strapped to our backs like mules. We started making our way up a wee path and wooden steps right up the face of the cliff which rose to 1,000 to 1,500 feet. It was scary, to say the least, but when the going got rough I got tough – or was it the other way around? It took us an hour climbing to the top and then when the passengers started to ascend, some of us had to go down again to give assistance.

The time was now about 10 pm and it was as clear as noon. Having got all our passengers up, we set off then on a mile hike which took us through a herd of possibly 1,000 reindeer and a Laplander camp. They thought we were strange people – the Laplanders, I mean, not the reindeer. By the time we got out to our destination at the other end of the headland, it was time to set up our picnic. At 11.45 pm the sun was almost touching the horizon with still a wee gap, big enough to put your hand in it but closing by the minute. The air was silent except the odd grunt of the reindeer and the cry of the curlew or seagull. Then the sun caught up with the horizon, they kissed for a moment, as one day was taken up on another. Then after a couple of minutes they parted company again until the next night. We stayed there for about an hour and then made our way back again, still in broad daylight. It was simply marvellous. By the way, we left one of our engineers behind us and since we were only a few short miles from northern Russia, the story went out that he defected as his father had done the previous year. It could be a yarn but he went missing, that's for sure.

This trip was known as the North Cape cruise and it lasted four weeks, starting from New York on 1 or 2 June when the sun was coming near its peak in the northern hemisphere. The average age of passenger was fifty to sixty years and they were a nice class of people into the bargain and had a bit more life in them than on some cruises. It was also a change from South America and Africa that we had seen so much of. Everybody here had a blond look about them and the scenery was so fresh and green.

I forgot to mention that we picked up a pilot in Reykjavik and he stayed with us until we got to Oslo. I can tell you he was needed, for some of the fiords we took in were narrow enough. It was like sailing along ceilingless corridors that would suddenly turn at right angles. The walls were a couple of hundred feet high and looked sheer. If you stared closely you might be able to pick out a wee house in a niche in the rock face, half-way up or down, whichever way you are coming, and in the water below a wee tiny rowing-boat would be tied to a jetty. There didn't seem to be any visible way down to the boat. These fiords lent themselves to photography, for the passengers were vying with each other for a place on the decks. I've never seen so many cameras in one place. Some had as many as five, which led me to believe that they were filming for camera clubs and such. Fare paid, eh? Sailing down from the North Cape, visiting Hammerfest, Trondheim, Bergen and a plethora of wee ports in between, as well as going in and out of the fiords, I

171

have never witnessed scenery like it, except in one other place, between the two islands of New Zealand called the George and Thompson sounds. The scenery was breathtaking, the narrow fiords had waterfalls cascading down, with the sun making rainbows through them. It was really the best time of the year to visit and the Yanks had it to a tee. Some of the fiords are three miles deep and the water was crystal clear. You could only marvel at the way the crew turned the ship with so little to spare. You could almost touch the land as she turned. It was exciting when going up one of these fiords to turn a corner and find a wee fishing village.

I did five of these cruises and I would do more if I had the chance. I can recall one night sitting on the dock in Oslo, waiting for the ship's boats to come back for us, when the shrimp boats came in and sold us shrimps just freshly cooked, and, boy, they tasted good.

We stayed at Oslo for a couple of days and then on to Göteborg and Stockholm. We moved from Copenhagen back out through the Skagerrak en route for Edinburgh, up round Scapa Flow and down to Oban. Then home to Bangor, County Down, Dun Laoghaire and Southampton. I met my family both in Bangor and Dun Laoghaire – as a matter of fact it was in Bangor that I proposed to Agnes and thank God she said OK and that was that!

ALL ASHORE THAT'S
GOING ASHORE

My next cruise took me into the Mediterranean, which we did twice a year, spring and fall. I got kind of used to the same ports, for over the years I had in all at least a dozen trips into the Mediterranean, starting from New York and crossing the Atlantic to Casablanca in Morocco. It was quite an experience going through the kasbah or native market place but I didn't like it very much, for everybody was wrapped up in big blankets and I wasn't sure what was going on underneath them. Maybe they had knives or guns, for they gave you the impression that they always seemed to be smuggling something or other. I was glad I didn't have to eat the food, for it was handled too much for my liking and it looked awful; but then again I was spoiled. Casablanca was a one-day visit and here a lot of overland tours were organised. It was common enough to 'lose' your passengers for eight or ten days. After Casablanca came Tangier, which was much the same except that we had an overnight stay there and then on to Gibraltar and into the Mediterranean.

We sailed along the North African coast, taking in all the ports as we went and sending passengers overland on scenic tours and picking them up elsewhere a few days later. A lot of the ports were familiar in name to me, for as I said at the start of this story, this is where the boys landed back in 1940 and I was hearing all the news from my pals at home. We had a pretty good boxing team on board and we were lucky to get a fight in Alexandria. This was a gala night with the crew and passengers for support. I could say I was carried out of the ring shoulder high but that would sound like a brag. What the hell! I was carried out and it caused a wee bit of a commotion, for it was the Egyptians that carried me out and our lads thought I'd come to grief, but no. It was their way of acknowledging the fact that I helped my opponent to his feet after he 'fell' out of the ring in the second round. I knocked him out in the third. The crowd were more than nice.

I regret now that I didn't take the opportunity to go to the Pyramids on one of the organised trips but I thought I'd seen enough and kept saying, 'next time' – and it never happened. Our next call was Port Said at the mouth of the Suez Canal and then we moved up to Haifa in Israel. The first time we went there we had to anchor out in the bay as there were no harbour facilities. It was during the exodus of Jews from war-torn Europe to the motherland. A movie was made about it with Paul

Newman in the lead. I saw these people come in, from somewhere, in small crafts like half-deckers, with all their belongings in the boats. There would be two or three generations of them with what appeared to be sheep or goats tied to the rails. As they landed they were taken and catalogued and a big label tied round their necks. They were then marched off to a camp not unlike the prison camp that some had not so very long ago been liberated from. Looking back now, I realise it must have been frightening for them. They were kept in these camps until they were processed and shipped out to a kibbutz. These are collective farms and they have helped make Israel the country it is today. When I was in New York I noticed huge ads on every hoarding and on the subway, all over the place, demanding that you 'Help Israel.'

We took a trip to Bethlehem and saw the birthplace of Christ and the slab or table in Jerusalem where the Last Supper was eaten. It was a lovely experience but I felt you couldn't take all they were saying to you too seriously and you had to take some things with a pinch of salt. On the drive to Bethlehem I couldn't help but notice the huge water sprinklers that were irrigating the desert and how industrious the people were. The Israeli pound wasn't worth the paper it was printed on outside of Israel and the American dollar was the flag of all nations, so things ashore were cheap as long as you had dollars. I remember being called on with about six other stewards to clear out the ship's bars, of which there were about ten, and dump all the empty bottles ashore. After wrestling and carrying on like a gang of schoolboys, we got the bottles down to the working gangway, ready to go ashore. While we were sitting chatting about our escapades and goings-on the previous night, what was on line for the night and so forth, this local Israeli asked us what we were going to do with the bottles, to which some wag answered, 'We'll sell them to you.' Your man rose to the bait and says, 'I'll give you 500 pounds for them.' Naturally we nearly took his hand off but that's when we really found out the value of the Israeli pound, for I think my 100 pounds bought me a postcard and a stamp home.

Now, the next time there about six months later was a totally different story, for there was a new pier to go alongside, the camps were gone and all the rolling stock along the quayside had 'made in USA' stamped all over them. America really pulled out all the stops and put them on their feet, that's for sure! The country has kept growing.

I have never been to Beirut and I regret that, for I'm told it is a beautiful city; instead we made our way to Istanbul in Turkey. On the way up the Dardanelles one of the lecturers gave a talk on the now famous First World War blunder blamed on Churchill. If my memory serves me right, a quarter of a million Allied troops (particularly the Anzacs) lost their lives there. I looked that day at the surrounding cliffs and realised that the soldiers were being asked to do the impossible, for the Turks had the high ground and just under the water were rolls of barbed wire that tangled up the landings. The Turks shot them like ducks in a barrel. Our ship's flag got another dropping to half-mast and we sailed on up to Istanbul. It was here I visited two continents on one day simply by crossing a bridge: I went from Europe into Asia and back.

On to Athens where tours were laid on for the Acropolis and other places of interest. We then made our way to Sicily, where we ran aground in the Strait of Messina and had to send up the coast for a navy tug to pull us off at high tide. Palermo was very quaint with wee cafés along the streets and what looked like a family of Mafia at every table eyeing everybody up. It was here the maestro came from the music school and played the church organ for us. This organ, the second biggest in Europe, had 6,000 stops and it was only the maestro who played it and then only on special occasions; this was one of them. It was brilliant.

Our next stop was Naples and here I saw Lucky Luciano, the Mafia boss of New York who was jailed for murder and drugs some years before in the States. He cut a deal with President Roosevelt before the Americans invaded Sicily and his part of the deal was to have his Sicilian 'family' make things easy for the landings by sabotaging the German war effort. For this he would be freed from prison in the United States but would be deported to Sicily with a proviso that he wouldn't leave the island. So much for the proviso: I saw him in a restaurant in Naples with his two bodyguards and a girlfriend. It was like an old black-and-white gangster movie. First the two bodyguards came in and looked the place over and then he came in with the girl and sat at a table apart from his lackeys, though they jumped to light his fag for him. I asked the waiter who he was, and he said Lucky Luciano. I said, 'I thought he wasn't supposed to leave Sicily', and his reply was 'He has more money than the whole Italian government put together, so he can do what he pleases.'

I had an old guy on another cruise with me and I knew to look at the wife that she came out of the chorus line. God love her, she was real 'brassy' and she sat on his deaf side and talked away to me about her time in showbiz. I knew he had found her in one of the chorus lines by her talk. He was a rough diamond all right, about seventy-five to her thirty-five years and he ran a seafood house up in the Catskills in New York state. There he hosted the Mafia 'family' gatherings when they cut up the states into territories for the rackets. Before he left he gave me a list of hotel people in Las Vegas and Reno to look up if I ever wanted a job.

In Naples we got trips to Sorrento and along the Amalfi drive to Pompeii and took in a visit to a factory making cameos. I bought a couple of them as they were all the go back then. Agnes still has them in some drawer or other. Although I wasn't all that far from Rome I never ever visited that city. Odd, wasn't it, since I went to Naples so many times?

I forgot to mention Dubrovnik in Yugoslavia which at that time was behind the Iron Curtain and though the buildings were nice the whole place seemed so drab. I often wondered what the attraction for the passengers was. Maybe it was to remind themselves how well off they were, eh? After Dubrovnik we crossed the Adriatic to Venice and one of the things that caught my attention, or was it my imagination? was while sailing up the Grand Canal to anchor opposite St Mark's Cathedral, the buildings all looked tilted. I loved Venice and had a few runs on the gondolas. Josef Locke had a big hit a few short years before with 'Hear My Song, Violetta', so I'm sure the gondoliers were fed up listening to it. St Mark's Cathedral and the Doge's Palace were the places to see, and since Venice is renowned for its glass, a conducted tour of a glass factory was in order. I was always mesmerised by their skill.

There was always the call to Pisa, where I got a lean over the tower and then round to San Remo and hence to the highlights of the Riviera, Nice, Monaco and Cannes. From what I see on television and magazines it's clear that they've all changed for the worse. In the 1950s there wasn't a building over three storeys high and it was here the middleclass English came. I'll always keep in my mind the sight of the *Caronia* lying in the little bay just round the corner from Cannes. It was like a picture postcard and, as I said, she was painted two shades of green with a white superstructure and red, white and black funnels. As the surrounding country is all hilly, the roads winded and twisted round to give you a fantastic view down into the little bay with the ship in the middle, as if posing for photographers. I had a trip round the casino in Monte Carlo; just a visit, no

178

gambling. On then to Marseille and Barcelona, where the architecture was beautiful and the town gorgeously set. I only hope they haven't overdeveloped it as in so many other places. We took in Palma in the Balearics and Ibiza and looking back now, I realise that there wasn't a high-rise hotel in sight. Oh, how they have spoiled that part of the world!

From there to Valencia, Almería, Málaga and out again to Gibraltar; up the coast of Portugal to Cádiz and then Lisbon, Bilbao and home through the Bay of Biscay. It was here the passengers used to be nervous about hitting bad weather. Strange, every time I went through it it was like a duck pond. Whilst I loved New York and was always thrilled sailing up the Hudson, I looked forward too to the Solent, passing the Nabbs to berth beside one of the two *Queens*, whichever one would be in dock at the time. And there was always the possibility of a trip home to Derry.

The journey from Southampton home was long but from London up to Heysham there was a good chance of meeting someone from Derry on their way home too and it didn't seem as long any more. One night in particular I fell in with Shan Orr, a neighbour's wean, and could he sing! He was great! He sang all of Nelson Eddy's repertoire and after a wee bit of lubrication he got into what might be known in the Isle of Doagh as 'grand order'. People came from both directions to hear him and we got the whole list. He was in great voice that night and, as another Derryman, I was proud of him. Shan had a natural baritone voice but like a couple of other Derry artistes I knew, he was too happy at home, and wouldn't exert himself. Otherwise he could have carved out an international career.

Jews don't celebrate Christmas, so a big number of New York Jews chartered the ship for a fifteen-day cruise to the Indies every year. I would have my holiday in October back in Derry when I would decorate the house with Christmas

179

decorations and put up a Christmas tree. Then I would sail out in early November for six months' cruising. It took me quite a few years to realise that my family was going to grow up without me, and as soon as I caught on to this I quit the sea for ever. Agnes was expecting our first child and I was on the American west coast finishing a South Pacific cruise when one of my passengers, a Mrs McCarton, asked me what I thought of southern California. When I expressed an off-the-cuff opinion about it, she invited me out with my family to her home in Los Angeles. I told her my wife was expecting her first baby and she said, 'Bring her out and have the baby in the hospital', a hospital with eighty beds which she owned lock, stock and barrel.

I reckoned at the time, she is having a good time on the cruise but when she gets back to dry land and her own world, I, Agnes and my family will be forgotten. Not so, for two years later I put her to the test and surprisingly she soon set the wheels in motion and I set sail (I should say I flew) to Los Angeles as an emigrant. While waiting for my emigration papers to be processed I came ashore and took a job with the British admiralty as a civilian steward in one of their camps outside the town. Derry at this stage had become a naval garrison, and all naval establishments were named after old sailors or battles. I thought it was a load of old tripe but that's naval tradition for you, so who was I to argue? My camp was called the Anson site, and going into work in the morning I went 'on board' and coming out at night I came 'ashore'. Did you ever hear such nonsense? Anyway, I knew I was only going to be a short time there, so I bit my lip and as with other fixes I was in before, I enjoyed myself. The Anson site, I should tell you, was made up by a number of huts linked together and left over from the war. I think the Yanks built them and then after the war the Royal Navy took them over.

My old boxing buddy Gerry McCauley – 'Red' McCauley was his boxing name – and myself made a quare team, for anybody over forty to us was ancient and we got up to all kinds of devilment. Red was a good waiter too and the two of us were assigned to the captain's table, where we worked with the regular navy men known as 'killicks'. (The word means 'anchors'.) The Suez Crisis was in full swing, for Colonel Nasser, the Egyptian President, had ousted King Farouk in a bloodless coup and closed the Suez Canal which had been controlled by the British. Nasser had no love for the British since the days of his military training in England, where he was slighted and now he was going to make them pay. That's a simplistic explanation – I'm sure it ran deeper – but I'll settle for that now. This meant all shipping had to round the Cape of Good Hope which added an extra 4,000 or 5,000 miles. This put the squeeze on the oil trade and was one of the causes of the petrol rationing that was imposed in the UK. I mention this because one night at the captain's dinner the buffet table was laid up and I could see the killicks acting very strange. When the stench of petrol rose with the heat of the room it dawned on me that these fellows were out siphoning the officers' cars, bringing it in in buckets and storing it under the table. It was hair-raising to say the least, for if anything had gone wrong, everybody would have been very surprised. It would have been worse than the battle at Trafalgar. I think the guard at the gate looked on Red and myself with disgust, for we used to do a sailor's hornpipe past him going out and in.

I invested in a car, which was stupid, since I was preparing to leave the country any day, but for £5 it was a steal. I remember the dealer saying it was a '33 Austin and now I'm not so sure whether he said 1833 or 1933 but, anyway, I bought it. She was the type of car that Al Capone would have driven, with running boards, big headlamps up on the mudguards, the spare wheel fixed onto the back outside. She was painted a grey-blue, so I christened her *Bluebird* after Donald Campbell's world-speed-record-breaking car. Starting this car was a trick on its own, so I didn't worry if some ugly person would try to steal her. (Why do I insist calling her 'her'?) I had a lot of fun with her and although she may have always got you there, nine times out of ten you had to come back in the bus. But she was my very first car and I wish I had her now, for I'm sure she would be a collector's item. The stories about her are legend but I have to move on and all I can say is that I was sad to part with her. I just left it, an orphan on the street, and swanned off to America.

CITY OF ANGELS

My emigration papers came through, I made a reservation and flew away like a bird to Los Angeles. I left Agnes, Marina and Giovanni at home until I would have a place of our own for them to come to. Agnes was expecting our third child as well, so we thought it better all round for her to stay and have the baby at home. I left Derry in April 1957 and Fionnbarr was born on 22 August. The first I saw of him was on the runway of what is now LAX – Los Angeles International Airport. He was just a wee bundle in the air hostess's arms. The arrival was about midnight and in those days we were allowed right to the plane's gangway on the tarmac.

Los Angeles must have been a shock to Agnes that night as we drove to our new home. She had never seen so many neon lights or so many cars. At that time it was reckoned there were over five million cars in the Los Angeles area alone. The weans were sound asleep in the back of the Mercury and Agnes was in a dream as I showed off a wee bit, driving home. The car was new to me too, as I had only just bought it a day or two earlier.

A week before this I didn't even have a car and Mrs McCarton says to me, 'John, is it not about time you had your wife and children out here with you? What's the hold up?' I told her I was putting together the deposit for a car, their fares and a house. All that in six months, impossible! So she said, 'Is that all? Here, go out and see about a house and be careful of the district. Get near good schools and a church.' With that she signed a cheque and handed it to me. There was no amount written on it and whenever I drew her attention to this all she said was, 'Just whatever it takes.' I should mention at this time that she was a widow, a millionaire, and told me she had adopted me and my family. I didn't feel like getting adopted because I had a good enough mother. Did I not already tell you I was a mamma's boy? No kidding though, she was very kind to us.

I went out and bought the house and with whatever money I had I furnished it from the front door to the back, stocked the cupboards with baby foods and dried goods, cereals and such. Mrs McCarton took the drapes from her own apartment and got them hung professionally for me. I bought a new Early American bedroom suite with about six pieces in it. It had a four-poster bed and it put me in mind of the Isle of Doagh, only instead of bags of chaff on the slats there was a double sprung mattress. It didn't matter anyway, for in the middle of the night the bloody slats slipped and we finished up on the floor. Many's

184

a night the big chaff or straw beds would collapse with us too when we were kids. It brought back many memories. We were so happy; it was the first real time together without waiting to go back to sea and be separated again. Mrs McCarton sent us a full entertainment kit that you would see in any playground, with slides, swings, seesaw and a horse. The day it arrived, in crates, I was flabbergasted – even flummoxed – because it would have taken an engineer to understand the drawings and the instructions with it to put it together. It was some Meccano set, I can tell you! When we left California three years later I gave it to my next door neighbours, Pete and Marie, because they had children about the same age as ours.

By the way, that couple came from Derry too. He was Pete McFarland, nicknamed 'Spanky' in Derry and she was Marie Doherty, one of the gang that attended the wee club where I met Agnes, so it was a coincidence that we should meet again so far away from home. Pete had emigrated to America some years before, was conscripted and I think stationed in Germany with the Rhine army. I suppose he cut a quare dash in his American army uniform when he came home on leave. Anyway, he ups and marries his childhood sweetheart and takes her out to America with him. Now doesn't that sound nice!

About a week after I arrived in Los Angeles I was walking down the street from my apartment, whistling. (You know, you never hear people whistling nowadays and Derry used to be full of whistlers, especially the windowcleaners up the town in the mornings. God, it would do your heart good up Carlisle Road and Ferryquay Street to hear the Willis family: father and four sons, all windowcleaners, up and down ladders whistling away, all in tune too!) I was passing by this two-storey condominium, when the voice rang out, 'Johnny', and I was taken aback. I looked up and there was Marie on the upstairs balcony and the best of it was, I lived only across the street from her. We struck it up there and then and that friendship remained until I left California to come home.

When I bought the house Marie and Pete bought the one next door, so our fence was their fence and it was a lovely setup indeed. We were sorry to leave them when we decided to come back home. Sad to say that Marie died of leukaemia in her early forties. We were back in Derry when she died and some years later Pete visited home and we made contact. He didn't remarry, which was something, for his family, like my own, were quite young and could have done with a mother's care. He must have decided to raise the children himself. Fair play to him, for the Yanks are great ones for marrying people off. Pete just got a bit older like myself and his family are all married now. Seeing him again brought back memories of the sleepless nights I used to give him.

My first job in Los Angeles was in the Terrace Room in the Statler Hilton hotel. It was funny now when I look back. It was my first week living there and I was staying with Mrs McCarton at an apartment she had for her visiting medical staff and I got up this morning and looked out over the 'land'. She lived on the west side and the ground sloped nicely up or down – depends which way you are going. Anyway, from this vantage point I could look downtown to where all the action should be, and off I set like Dick Whittington, keeping the tall buildings in my sight. There were no church steeples to guide me, only a couple of ten- or twelve-storey buildings. I didn't want to get on a bus, for I wasn't sure where to ask for – no sense complicating things – so I walked and walked and walked, and boy I was tired, for the temperature was up in the nineties. I was right in my assumption that I would spot the Statler, for although the tall buildings were few in number, the hotel stood out, being 11 storeys high with 110 bedrooms and a plethora of function rooms. Looking it over and using one of Amos and Andy's best lines, I said, 'Dis must be da place!'

Now it seems there was a terrace room in all the Statlers, so I figured that was the place to work, for it was the nightclub and people have a different attitude to spending money in their leisure time. Besides, it would be more interesting. Luck was with me, for when I went to the personnel office and showed them my seaman's book, which, by the way, was my only reference, giving the name of the ship, position held, conduct and ability noted and signed by the captain after every voyage. They must have been really impressed, for I was started right away, joined the union and did a wee yes-or-no exam on food and wine and reported that evening for battle. I was used normally to taking care of eight people but now I'd got about forty and it took some running around. With the help of God and two wee sticks, I managed and I became quite good, so good that I was moved down to the centre ring where the diamonds and furs were. I can tell you now that it was my accent that did it. Somehow they loved the Irish accent and I couldn't get over this. I would put on a down-South or out-West brogue or even do a Maggy McCay accent for them, and they loved it. It was fun and I really loved it too. (And I made a lot of money along the way as well.)

The nightclub was just like in the old movies; big sixteen-eighteen-piece band, with all the top stars of the time appearing there. Each show was booked in for three weeks with two shows a night, so that by the time it was over, I knew every word and song and I even duetted with Nelson Eddy singing 'The Indian Love Call' and Allan Jones and 'The Donkey Serenade'. They didn't know this, but with the lights out nobody knew who was singing, so it all sounded the same. The waiters worked in pairs: one to do the actual serving, the other to greet and seat the customers, present the menu, take their drinks order, give them time to make their minds up and be ready to assist them in choosing the food. Most of the time people thought they were doing the choosing but I can tell you a good waiter has your mind made up for you from the start. The maître d' was a German, Vogel by name, and he couldn't understand my attitude to life and why I was so Irish. I asked him one time was he in the Hitler Youth and he evaded the question. It stopped his snide remarks about downtrodden Ireland and England, but with all that, we got on well, so much so that when I was leaving to go up to Hollywood to work, he said he was sorry to see me go and if it didn't work out I would be welcome back.

Before I leave the Statler I should point out that I also had a lunchtime job serving lunch by the pool which the white-collar workers of downtown Los Angeles frequented. You can imagine my surprise the first day there, whilst serving four of these yuppies in a booth, I turned away from the table only to be confronted by a girl in a fur coat above all things, which she opened to reveal herself scantily clad in underwear. At this I panicked and tried to cover her with my waiter's cloth, only to find out from the dining-room captain that she was a model from one of the shops in the hotel foyer. In Derry you did not get embarrassed, you just got mortified! Well that was me. To me the men viewing these models were a bunch of ould Jessies but to bring it up to modern-day language they were a pack of perverts.

Dean Martin was the whole rage at the time and he was involved in a restaurant on Sunset Strip called Dino's Lodge, where I got a job. It had a very big neon light in the shape of Dino's head outside the restaurant which was featured in a current television detective series, 77 *Sunset Strip*. It was a two-storey building and the detective agency up above the restaurant in the series was really a high-class model agency. People came from all over to see Dino's, hoping to catch a glimpse of the man himself or the series' carpark attendant Ed 'Cookie' Byrnes – a proper puke – and at cocktail hour from 5 pm to 6 pm it was bedlam at the bar with the yuppies – that name wasn't invented yet but they were yuppies – standing four and five abreast. As soon as it hit 6 o'clock it was as if somebody shouted 'Fire', for then the bar emptied. The bar was at least 100 feet long and this was handled by the best barmen I've ever come across. Just two of them, and boy could they move and mix drinks and talk. They were paid well above the union rate but they were well worth it. At about 8 pm the diners started to come in and then it really got interesting, for with all the stars of the day frequenting it, the house would be booked out.

Don't forget I'm back in the fifties, so there was a different race of talent. I'm talking now of the stars of yesteryear, Frank Sinatra, Eddie Fisher, Vic Damone, Sammy Davis Jnr, Lucille Ball, Edward G. Robinson, John Ireland, Jim Backus, George Raft, Gregory Peck, Humphrey Bogart, Spencer Tracy, and others too numerous to list. I got to know them all, for many of them would ask for me and I would give them plenty of silly chatter. I hope I am not sounding bigheaded but two waiters were willing to break up their team if I would work with them. Now, this may sound strange to you but I want to point out that these were French waiters, trained on the Continent, so they were well qualified and it was indeed an honour to get this proposal – behind each other's back, I might add. The training in the old *Queen* stood me in good stead, but the Irish twang, brogue, call it what you may, was the secret of the game.

Franchot Tone was a big disappointment, for in the movies he used to look a real glamour boy, but when I saw him up close across a table, his nose was flatter than mine. I got mine boxing, so I wonder what his excuse was. I saw Lucille Ball so often on television that I was calling her Lucy at the table but she was

189

a lovely person and I was disappointed when she broke up with Desi Arnaz, for they seemed a nice couple – but that's Hollywood! I specially liked George Raft, for he looked good in real life, just what you would expect, and he always had a couple of ladies with him. He dressed immaculately and above all was a very good tipper, to me anyway.

There was always a gossip columnist present at a table where they could be seen. I always thought they were social vultures living off other people's misfortunes, always taking notes. I remember one night in particular plugging a phone into Vic Damone's table where he was sitting with a model – she was like one anyway – and the call was from his wife. She was phoning from the airport 3,000 miles away in New York to say she was leaving and taking the kids to Europe. He started to cry; can you beat that? Well, that was about midnight, and when I quit work two hours later there it was in the paper: 'Pier Angeli leaves Vic, takes kids to Europe.' And now we are worried about 'press and cabinet leaks' here. We're only playing at it.

I should mention that we fed about ten motor-cycle cops in the space of a night, for they came in twos and freeloaded their dinner. It was an unofficial protection racket and though they ate in the kitchen they sat down to it and got the whole works.

The maître d' at Dino's was called Luigi, first-generation Italian-American and he was in his last year of study as a Jesuit when he quit. Boy, could he recite the scriptures and papal bulls; he was in a class of his own. He was very good at languages, Italian Greek, French, Latin and a couple of Middle Eastern ones as well. I heard him myself, not that that would make it gospel but he could sure pass himself. The only thing was, he became anti-Church and would slag me for my beliefs. He was a good scout though and we got on like a house on fire, and I have the privilege of being the only waiter re-employed there, with the credit going to him for it.

THE KID'S LAST FIGHT

I worked hard in California and at one stage I had three jobs. I cooked breakfast in Mrs McCarton's hospital from 7 am to 10 am. You see, if you think you can do it, do it, for I got away with it and I didn't tell any lies. I just wasn't asked if I could or could not. The cook fell out with the full-time chef and I stepped in to help out. I was installed as breakfast cook. I used to say, 'God, if my ma could see me now!' – there I was, dressed up like a doctor, with a wee Benny hat, a mask hanging round my neck and white coat and pants. I looked just like Dr Kildare.

After cooking the breakfast for patients and staff, about 80 to 100 people, I would go and burn the stuff out of the operating theatre. I enjoyed the fun here, for a couple of nurses would set to and scrub me up like I was going in to operate. Instead I would lift my bucket and walk outside to the incinerator. One or two new doctors actually called me Doc and do you know, if they'd have asked me I'm sure I would have given them a hand in the theatre. That's power!

I used to take my uniform home with me and dress there because I was always late in the morning. One day as usual rushing to work I went through a red light – they all look the same, red lights, I mean. Anyway, I looked in my rear-view mirror and there they were, the cops, hot on my tail. I pulled in to the side and the cop got out, came back to me and greeted me: 'Well, Doc. You in a hurry?' I said, 'Yes, officer', all civil. No lies. He then asked me where I was going and I told him to the Rose Hospital. With that he gives me back my licence and says, 'Follow me!', jumps into his own car, turns on the siren, and with his lights flashing, speeds off with me in hot pursuit. God it was great, for all the traffic comes to a halt for fire brigade, ambulance and police, and there was I getting a clear run through, doing my best to keep up with these crazy cops. We pulled into the parking lot and I was shaking like a leaf. I locked my car and called to the cops, 'Thank you very much, officer', and I can hear them yet saying, 'Any time, Doc.' Little did they know that five minutes later I would be knee-deep in pots and pans, cooking breakfast.

After cooking the meal and having gone through the charade of the scrub up and the incinerator caper, I would then head downtown to the California Club, where I served lunch from 11 am to 1.30 pm. I had since changed my lunchtime job at the Statler. It was here in the California Club that I served Paul Getty, a very wealthy man by any standards, and the last meal

I served there was at the signing of contracts to redevelop downtown Los Angeles. The figure in the papers that evening was 150,000,000 dollars, and after having served the brandy and cigars, as I was closing the doors of the private dining-room the contracts were already on the table for signatures. At the table were ten bankers or developers and ten lawyers but since they didn't want my signature it was pointless my staying any longer, so I withdrew. Funny thing – that was in 1959 and in 1984 when Giovanni and Siobhán went out to the Olympics I asked them to look up the big hotel where I had worked. I gave them a very full description: eleven storeys high, second tallest building, right in the middle of downtown LA, so they couldn't possibly miss it. Well, when they came home after being away three weeks, I eagerly asked them about the Statler and when they said they couldn't find it, it set me wondering about educating children and all. A couple of years later I got a trip out and I too got lost, for my pride and joy was only a wee henhouse stuck in the middle of shamrock and oblong-shaped glass towers, sixty and seventy storeys high. My faith in my weans was restored, but that's just a wee aside.

After serving whatever company you had and enquiring from the host, 'Is there anything else?' you closed the doors and let them get on with their business. God knows what it was, it could have been the Mafia but I didn't care, for I got on the freeway and sped home in time to pick up the family and take them down to the beach until about 5 pm. Then home again, got showered and up to Hollywood to what I called my 'regular' job in Dino's. This pace went on for about eighteen months and when I got the wee things I needed for the house and family, I cut back on the work. It suited me to do this and I was full of stamina. That's a good one! I felt so good that my physician, Dr Donohue, talked me into a comeback. They say old fighters always think they've another fight left in them. Well

I was one of those fighters. I had just turned twenty-eight and the Doc remarked how fit I looked. We got to talking and he told me he had a very good friend in the business that he would introduce me to when I was ready. As it was almost three years since I'd laced a glove, I took myself downtown to a gym, not realising that it was in the heart of the Watts district. It was like the Congo and I was Stanley, for I stood out like a sore thumb, the only white man around.

Watts is where the riot broke out over civil rights in America and, while that may seem a simple explanation, you can read up on it, for it has been well documented. When I appeared in the place everybody stopped and stared, so I spoke to an old negro who looked like he had been through the mill and had served his apprenticeship, an old ex-pug, and I told him I wanted to box. He laughed at me and they all joined in but I had it in my head that I would soon put the hyena laugh on the other side of their faces. This old guy became my second and he would help me bandage and tape my hands and keep an eye on my clothes and although we weren't on name terms I got by just the same. It's all right skipping, boxing your own shadow and punching bags that don't hit you back but you need the real thing, someone to hit you back and sharpen you up, and that's where sparring partners come in handy.

I wasn't there too long – maybe a couple of weeks – when it happened. Into the gym came four or five guys, all black naturally, and in the middle was the 'paycheck'. He was dressed all flashy and I can see him yet with his Frank Sinatra style hat – then the whole go; I think from the movie *The Tender Trap* – and in he breezed. What seemed like half a dozen got round him, to strip and dress him. It looked like something out of a movie and if I'd seen it in one, I would have laughed. As it turned out, this fellow was the lightweight champion of California and he was just fresh back from England where he

194

went the distance with Dave Charnley, the then British and Empire champion. He lost that fight on points. I asked the old second if I could spar with the champ and, you know, the hum and the hysterical laugh that went round the room made me feel a right chump. Let them laugh; Whitey was nobody's mug. When the other champ looked me over and decided to teach me a lesson I was set to make it backfire, so I boxed his ears off. I sparred with this 'champ' every day and besides doing him the world of good it was a tremendous help to me and meanwhile I was pestered with offers to fight in Mexico, Phoenix, in Los Angeles and Canada, but I turned them all down, for I was saving myself for this friend of Dr Donohue's.

After about three weeks I felt I was ready to meet Dr Donohue's friend. A date was set and I was given an address in Beverly Hills. The friend turns out to be a big-time lawyer, a mouthpiece for the Mafia, always on television defending some hood or other. His name was Paul Caruso. Everything out there is so formal – not like back home, where you can drop in anywhere any time – so when I came to the address I was passed from one office to another and yet another – still not there yet – and lastly into the inner sanctum where Paul Caruso was sitting behind a massive kidney-shaped desk. The decor of all these offices was out of this world and you could feel an air of opulence about the place He was dressed immaculately, white shirt, good tie, well-cut suit and two inches of cuff showing. He had Italian features, sallow skin and dark wavy well-groomed hair. He shook my hand, asked me to sit down and after the small talk about the colour of my red hair and the fighting Irish he asked me how good a boxer I was, how many fights I had and, most of all, how many did I win. I told him that as far as I could remember I had had about seventy fights and I lost four. I added, 'Don't take my word for it. Try me!' So he said, 'OK, if you are as good as you say you are, I can get you money like this', spreading across the table a contract for his boy Art Aragon who was to fight Carmen Basilio for the middleweight title. Aragon's share was 333,000 dollars. That in 1958 wasn't bad money at all, so a date was made in a professional gym in downtown LA. I appeared with my gear as if for a fight, for that is what it was going to be. I already had experienced something like this in Auckland during one of my cruises. I took my workmate Scotty with me as a mascot and to watch my clothes when I stripped. The place itself was like most professional gyms, dressing rooms with lockers – but no locks – toilets which were up to scratch, clean, tidy, smelling of disinfectant. It's surprising how many times a fighter goes to the toilet before a spar or a weigh-in, so it's a necessary part of the whole setup.

I got stripped, taped my hands up like hammers and started to loosen out. I mightn't have bothered. Scotty went into the ring area in the next room where I couldn't see what was going on and came back to report that my 'try-out' was in the ring waiting for me. At the ringside was a well-dressed guy wearing a homburg hat, spats and smoking a cigar. I knew by the description that the big time was here, so out I went, nodded to my potential backer and climbed into the ring, never thinking for a minute that it was for the last time in my career and I would never duck under the top rope again. My trial-horse – and he had a kick like a horse – was a fellow called Cisco Andrade, a Mexican good enough to have fought Sugar Ray Robinson and Joe Browne and that calibre a couple of years before but drink and women always interfered with his life and so, to cut a long story short, he caught me a lovely upper-cut into the rib cage and almost tore the top rib from the sheet. I was strapped up for three months and by the time I got the strapping off I'd forgotten all about boxing. That was the Kid's last fight; I licked my wounds and hung up my gloves. By the way, Scotty told me next day that as soon as I got hit and put up my hands, Caruso turned on his heel and walked straight out the door and out of my life. He didn't even look back, for nobody loves a loser. It was nice of Scotty to tell me. That's what friends are for, I guess.

I didn't get home from Dino's until pretty late each night (about 2 am) and everybody would be asleep. You could fire the proverbial cannon up the street. Now, there was this huge dog in a garden directly across the street from my house but, I should point out, it was behind a six-foot chain-link fence, so I felt safe enough. On entering the street I would cut out the engine of the car and let her glide in quietly. Now the game was on! I slipped out of the car, eased the door shut, locked it, tip-toed up to my own door, slipped the key into the lock and opened it; then turned around to face the dog, which incident-ally was watching my every move – a proper watchdog. Dogs are funny too; if you don't do anything rash or sudden you can get away with murder. After squaring myself up to the dog, I would flail my arms and make a muffled 'yeaheeh' at it and then all hell would break loose. The ould dog would go mad trying to get out at me but I would slip into the house leaving the whole street in an uproar. Childish, wasn't it?

I would then have my usual supper, a large bottle of coke and a gallon of chocolate ice cream, read the paper, watching cow-boy pictures on television all at the same time and unwind from the night's work. I would sit till about 4 am and then go to bed. Sure as your word, when I would meet Pete the next day he was bound to start on about the dog and the noise. 'Did you not hear it?' he would say, and naturally I would say: 'Naw, niver heard a thing', and he would say: 'I'm gonna get me a forty-five and blast that goddam dog.' After a couple of nights' respite I would do the same trick and, God love him, he never caught it on. My mother's comment on this sort of thing was, 'Little amuses the innocent.'

Mrs McCarton never did see the house she bought, though when I was leaving I made sure to sell it and I gave her back her money and any profit accrued in the sale. She didn't want to take it but I made her, for she had been much too kind. We visited often and she took it bad when we left America to come home, for she said herself that she had adopted me and my family as her own.

You might ask, why did we come home, when I was doing so well? Well, I'll tell you. It all came about one Sunday when a lot of Irish were gathered in Myles and Bridie Kyle's house in Long Beach and the conversation started about the old country, about times past and present. Everybody was going over the whole gambit of England having her boot in our throat, for – I think 900 years was mentioned. Well yours truly Daniel O'Connell Doran got up and made a speech. I said, pointing to the children playing on the floor, 'That's Ireland there and I've done her an awful dirty trick by taking those children out of it. I'm robbing the country of its future, so I am going back', and the very next day I put the house up for sale and booked Agnes and the weans on the plane back to Derry. It seemed drastic at the time but Agnes agreed with me wholeheartedly. There have been times since that I ask myself, 'Did I do right?'

After Agnes and the weans went home I sold the house and car, gave away our furniture to our friends and moved up to an apartment on Sunset Boulevard just walking distance from Dino's, where I knuckled down to a lonely life again. And it turned out to be the loneliest time of my life, for though I was living in the heart of Hollywood nobody from home knew I was there and I took a wild dread that I would not wake up some morning and nobody would find me for days. After a week or so at this I thought I may as well be at sea, so one day I hitched a ride down to Long Beach and joined the US Coast Guard. The Matson line was sailing out to Honolulu but I was so unsettled that just before I sailed I changed my mind, for it seemed I was going further away from home instead of nearer. I decided to work my way back and one morning I left Los Angeles for New York.

Arriving there I booked into a fleabag of a hotel just off Broadway and 49th Street because I wanted to be near the action – hotel work, that is. Realising that I would have to start going through the whole rigmarole of joining the union and all that sort of thing, I headed for the place I knew best – the docks – where the *Queen of Bermuda*, a British ship charted in American waters, therefore paying American rate, was doing handy fifteen-day cruises to the Bahamas and the West Indies. With my past experience on cruises I signed on as a first-class waiter. It was just what I needed and it was here I nearly entered show business.

A dance team with Gene Nelson, the star dancer of many big stage musicals and films, travelled down with us doing a travelogue film. It was customary that the crew put on a show and luau on the beach in Hamilton, Bermuda, and everybody was expected to perform, crew and passengers alike. So I started to act the eejit and after it was over Nelson and his agent asked me to meet them in New York with the idea of getting their writers to talk to me. When I got back to New York I never got in touch. Instead I phoned Los Angeles to Dino's because I still had a paycheck lying there. Luigi answered and said, 'Come on home.' I said, 'Are you serious?' and he repeated what he had said. So instead of sailing east to Ireland, I flew almost 3,000 miles west to California and was back in harness next night. I found another wee apartment with a swimming-pool five minutes' walk from Dino's, this time on Hollywood Boulevard and stopped there for about six weeks. Then one morning coming home from Mass I found a cable under the door saying my mother was dying. I got the first plane out to

New York. You know, I was beginning to feel like John Foster Dulles, the American Secretary of State at that time, and he was doing some flying!

Next morning I was back in Derry and the same taximen met me at the LMS station; again it seemed that nothing had changed and the town hadn't closed down after all when I left. On top of that I wasn't even missed but I thanked God anyway that I was home, back amongst my own people. After the reception and seeing my mother alive but going 'down the hill' very fast, I made my way to the dole just to register myself and the family back into the country again. At the end of the week I received £7.10s and four free pints of milk a day for the weans. I was on welfare for the first time in my life. All the big times had vanished but I wasn't despairing in any way, for I'm a great believer in the old saying, 'When one door closes behind you, another will open in front of you...' or something like that. And so it did for me.

A DERRY LANDLUBBER

Three years before, as I was taking the train out of Derry to the airport in Antrim, I saw men breaking ground for the site which Du Pont occupies today and little did I know that I would be back there in time for start-up. I was asked by an acquaintance who worked in the personnel office to apply for a job and since I had no knowledge of chemicals or engineering, I thought that I might get a job in a catering capacity: setting up meetings and working lunches for the higher ups. It would seem that I was creating a job for myself and it would be a grand cushy wee number just taking care of the big wigs. I was so sure that they would have had that sort of setup, but, no. My application was in and I intimated that was what I was interested in and once again my seaman's book was the only reference or CV that I had. It came to my aid again for the personnel officer was an ex-Royal Navy man and when he saw the names of the ships I'd sailed on he thought I was William Bligh or James Cook – a real deep-water type.

I couldn't go wrong with this fellow; as he said, 'Any man who has sailed on the two *Queen*s and gone round the world like you is my man.' To make a long story short, a Colonel Davidson, who was your man's lackey or office boy, was asked to give me an aptitude test and I was taken into another room and handed a question sheet with thirty or forty 'yes' or 'no' questions on it. He placed a stopclock on the table in front of me and after so many minutes when the bell on it rang I was supposed to lay down my pen and stop writing. Off he went and the first thing I did was to stop the clock, and then start into the questionnaire. Now I've done football coupons many a time before and since but never had the same luck. I used the same method: I marked the paper with two yeses, three nos and so forth. When I was finished I started the clock up again and the wee bell rang. I would say more than twenty minutes elapsed rather than the five or was it ten minutes allotted and the colonel came back and picked up my paper. Then I was taken back to the personnel manager to continue our saga at sea, round the China Station, as they say in Navy circles.

Now comes the big picture, the funny part. The colonel comes back after checking my paper, places it in front of the personnel officer – just as we were sinking the Japanese cargo fleet in Madagascar – and I can hear his answer yet. When asked, 'How did he do?' he replied, 'He did terribly well.' I'm sure there was a slight pause between 'terribly' and 'well' so I waited.

'Just what I expected', was the manager's reply, and I was offered a job to train as a chemical operator which, of course, I accepted and left the catering behind me for a while.

It was strange that I should be among the first batch of twenty employed to commission and run the plant that I had seen begun three years previously. That was over thirty years ago. It was a very drastic change for me, a real culture shock, but I took up the challenge and at the time of my departure eighteen months later I was told I was in line for promotion. It was good crack at the start, for we were all greenhorns and since the building wasn't completed we were sent to a classroom for sixteen weeks to learn all about the system and the maze of pipes that the plant was made up of. After the plant was handed over to us from Construction and we had a few dummy runs with water instead of chemicals we were put on shifts with the real thing. It was all very exciting, for by this time we had a fair idea of what we had been trained for and as this plant was built specially for us and as we were the first to run it, there was a great sense of pride in the air. That was as well as the very obnoxious smells we created. We were making neoprene, a synthetic rubber, and it was being shipped all around the world. The operators – that's us – had to report fifteen minutes before the start of the shift for a handover from the previous shift, and at the start it was a really mucky, wet, dirty job.

On the 4 pm-to-midnight shift and the midnight-to-8 am I used to come in dressed in my waiter's gear as if I had been to a party and I would take my handover dressed like a tailor's dummy. Some of the boys would look at me strange and say, 'You're not going to do much work dressed like that', and I'd dismiss it, saying, 'Don't worry; I'll be OK.' As soon as they went home I'd run down like the clappers to the change-house and pull on the old glad rags and water boots. Then after fighting the 'elements' – I want to keep it chemical – all night, about a half-hour before the shift finished, I would nip down again to the change-house and dress up for the oncoming shift, who would look at me strange, saying, 'Not much work done last night, eh!' It was a mucky job and dangerous too, for I saw a man killed one morning and a workmate and me were the last persons he spoke to. He asked us directions, we pointed to the apparatus in question and seconds later it blew up. We both were not more than twenty yards from him. Thank God no one has died since. Du Pont's safety record before and since was above reproach. They were very safety conscious.

One day the Du Pont gate was left open and I got out, and where do you think I headed? Where but to Southampton, where I joined the *Queen Mary* in the first-class dining-room. On arrival in Southampton after a five-year absence I had to send my seaman's papers to London and this meant a delay of three weeks but the luck of the Irish was with me again. The shore superintendent was coming down the gangway after having finished his business when he spotted me and asked 'What are you doing here?' I told him my papers were being processed, so he said, 'Get your gear and sign on going down the river', which is what I did for she sailed within the hour. It was nice to know that I was remembered after five years' absence and, on top of that, when I reported for duty that first dinner I was given a good station in the middle of the room.

The restaurant manager was Cyril Wareham whose father was a bedroom steward on the *Titanic* and he got a mention in a book named *A Night To Remember* about her first and last voyage and how she struck an iceberg and sank. Cyril's father gave someone his lifejacket and went down with the ship and Cyril got a job with the company for life as a token of gratitude. He was my boss on the *Caronia* five years previously and was also a great boxing fan of mine. He didn't forget me and I was put into the centre of the dining-room right away, for that is where the money is. I remember going up the gangway on sailing day to New York saying to myself how selfish it was of me to leave Agnes to rear the family on her own – we now had six children – and it was about time that I measured up to my responsibilities. I knew then I had made another of my many mistakes but since I'd made my bed I thought I'd better lie in it till I came up with another harebrained idea.

It so happens that one of the American personnel from Du Pont, Bill Carden, who was my supervisor and taught me the little I know about chemical plants, was going back home after two years commissioning the plant, and that night at dinner he was allotted to my station. By the way, Bill died in an explosion in the Wilmington plant shortly after. He was easily the bravest man I have ever met, and I make no exception, for on the morning of the explosion at Du Pont Bill showed his true colours. I can see him yet running towards what could have been certain death to turn off valves to stop the after-fire blowing up three very volatile tanks. The details I won't bore you with but Bill knew what he was doing and knew the danger attached. In my mind he was great; some bravery is a spur of the moment thing and no real thought goes into it but this case was different, for Bill knew what the consequences could have been.

Sorry I digressed, but I had to say that about Bill, may he rest in peace. It was a nice pleasant voyage, and he had his family with him – typical American boy and girl, and his wife. I must have turned on the charm, for Bill wrote back to the plant and suddenly I found myself doing welfare officer for Du Pont, as all the Americans where starting to go home and leave the plant to the locals. Now, I was at sea to earn money and I can tell you there was no money from this kind of passenger as they were all on a budget. Though I got tips, it wasn't what I was accustomed to, and the restaurant manager, thinking he was doing me a favour by giving me these people, had to be wised up. I had to have a word in his ear to give me a by.

The shipping scene had changed, for planes were now in the air and everybody was in a hurry. Why should you take six days to New York when you could fly in six hours? By the end of the season in late September 1961 we sailed back from New York with twenty-five people in the first-class dining-room, which had seating for 750 passengers. They could have all sat together at the one table. The other ships were affected the same way and the writing was on the wall for ships of passage and the catering staff that go with them. I had a long weekend in Southampton, so I invited Agnes over to see what kind of life I was having. I'm sure she saw as many 'big ships' in that couple of days that she would want to look at in a lifetime but we had a nice holiday and we were together. I made up my mind that I would come home to stay.

Again I was more than lucky, for I was home about a week when I got a call from Du Pont offering me my old job back, so I started back to work. After a couple of uneventful years as an operator I began to look at the lab technicians and noticed that they were always dressed in lovely clean white coats. I enrolled in the Strand tech, doing, or should I say, reading, maths, physics and chemistry O levels, thinking I needed at least those qualifications. I applied for a change to the lab and was accepted, but the funny thing about it was, I needn't have wasted my time at the tech, for a monkey trained long enough could have done the job. All the samples for analysis were done by numbers. Every now and again there used to be classes of schoolboys or schoolgirls shown round the lab and I would go in to my wee act and have my own demonstrations behind the supervisor's back. The carbon ice in the coloured water went a bomb for me and the pupils gave me more attention than the guide. I know, I know; it was a clear case of bad example.

One of the lab techs had spent a while studying pharmaceutical chemistry and for some reason or other didn't finish the course but he had the gift of the gab and the uneducated like myself hung onto his every word. He was a wizard at making hair shampoo and I stumbled onto making glue, so anything that needed glueing was stuck with my own concoction. There were bottles of glue lying round the house for years after I left Du Pont. My time in the lab was enjoyable and before long I was attached to a chemist whose job was to troubleshoot the process, which took him and me out to the plant, or field, as it was called. Here I was useful to him because I knew my way about out there and he could rely on me to take readings and observations over a period of weeks at a time. I was supposed to climb iron ladders up three and four storeys in wet and windy weather (sometimes blowing hurricanes) to take a reading that I already knew. Because I had been trained in that building I could tell by the sound, so I always had a good guess – one of Bill Carden's old tricks; he used always to say, 'Listen!'

Well, I gathered all this data and it was then sent up to a computer at Queen's in Belfast, where I pictured a big room full of tapes and discs and whirligigs and such, all working like mad, waiting to chew up all the information I was collecting. So every now and again I thought I'd set them a poser and give in a bum reading. Now, all these readings, pressures, temperatures, vacuums and readings from charts in the control room, would be jotted down and reported back to the chemist and the poor guy's nose would bleed profusely when one of the readings was askew. I figured that it was good for his blood pressure, you know, the sudden loss of blood and all that; so every now and again I used to give him the odd 'outside' reading, to keep his pressure right. He was a good scout though, for he put a letter of recommendation in my file. I often wondered what happened to the computer in Queen's, for I was hoping to send it mad. I pictured it jumping up and down with smoke belching out of it.

Just before the bug hit me again, I was asked to assist in a transfer of the lab library to the office block – known then as 605 building – and it was here that the chemists kept their files. From time to time one of these chemists would leave the plant and his files or projects would be handed on to his replacement and the new man would use it for reference. That sounds OK, except that I, being an avid comics reader, had a pile of comics to dispose of, so where better than into these files. I often wondered what they thought of each other when looking up some reference and finding a *Beano* or *Dandy* or *Rover*. I also put a comic under the blotters around the big new conference or board table, which was able to seat over a dozen. I would have loved to have been around to see the expression on their faces when turning over their blotting pads and finding comic cuts. Maybe they enjoyed it.

The bug did hit me again and as I had given Du Pont almost ten years of my life, I decided enough was enough, so I bought myself a mobile fish and chip van, which I designed myself, and left the plant. The van was an immediate success and Agnes and the older children helped out at the weekends. We worked mostly within a twelve mile radius of the town, in little housing estates of about sixty or so houses. There were lots of these wee hamlets and we were a novelty but the food was good into the bargain. It must have been good, for we had the same customers from day one and it was instant cash. At the end of the week I didn't have to divide with anybody but just pay my bills for goods used. It was just like the old days at sea, making plenty of money.

I met many a queer person along the road and one wee man, I remember, used to come out of the pub at night when I stopped in Claudy village. (This featured in a terrible explosion in 1972 when eight people died.) You'd hear him grunting his way down the street to the van and he was so full he couldn't speak.

I just fed him the fish suppers and not a word was spoken until he had eaten six or seven suppers. Then he would leave his money up on the counter for me to take whatever he owed and off he would stagger home, a journey of about four miles.

Another fellow would meet me outside the Railway Bar at Eglinton and buy ten double fish. One night, thinking they were for a gang of workers as there was a huge warehouse near-by, I asked him if he wanted them wrapped separately. 'Fuck a bit of it!' he says. 'I'll eat them as they are.' Another fellow used to buy a load of fish and I always threw in a few bags of chips free until one night I just happened to say, 'The children like the fish then, eh?' and he said, 'Naw, these are for the cats.'

TROUBLES

When the Troubles started on 5 October 1968, like lots of others I got involved and went on the streets to protest. I think amongst other things we wanted better opportunities for the young in Catholic colleges, who were coming out with an education but getting menial jobs below their capabilities, whilst the better jobs were being kept for the Protestants. It was the same in housing. One day the bubble burst and we all took to the streets. Now, that is a very simple way of telling it and no doubt some writers or historians have gone into more detail, but suffice it to say that's how it started. Happening so publicly on the streets, it was foolhardy of me to think I would escape the civil rights campaign. During the day I was engaged in sit-downs and street protests and then at night I parked my van outside the Orange hall, selling fish and chips. It was only a matter of time before they would get to me and so they did, with a vengeance. I didn't think it would be so vicious though.

All this time I had backed John Hume and for this I make no apologies because I believed he had the solution and I am proud to say I was his election office manager at his first attempt for a seat in Stormont.

I'm still backing John Hume. Who else? But before I leave the civil rights saga, I would like to tell you one or two true stories. I got involved not for patriotic reasons but because it seemed to be the thing to do at the time. When I was asked to come to Duke Street on that eventful Saturday, 5 October 1968, I was too busy with my own life but as the stories began to filter back into the town of the batterings the marchers got, the old blood started to boil and the job of defending Ireland in her time of need once again became a reality. Bill Craig banned all marches and assemblies, so people took it on themselves to break the ban. The following Monday it was broken literally dozens of times. Dockers – we had docks then, alas all gone now – marched out to the Guildhall Square, and factory girls would suddenly down tools and walk out and march to the square and march back again. All kinds of wee businesses would just up and out, all marching to the square, or better still to the war memorial in the hallowed ground inside Derry's walls, and just stand about and then march back.

It was a great time of togetherness and the message to Bill Craig was loud and clear. There are a lot of wee stories – some printed others not – of things that happened. One comes to mind. Dicky Valley was a well-known and likable character in

Derry. Everybody knew Dicky and at this time he lived in a wee house in St Columb's Wells. The street was built right under the Derry walls and during the July and August parades round the walls, the Orangemen would catcall and throw pennies and ha'pennies down at the Catholics below. This is fact, not propaganda, and it was down this wee street with its population of poor enough people, mostly well on in years, who were just putting in their days, that a crowd of drunken policemen and B Specials ran amok and battered in their windows and doors. It was sheer terror and the elderly people were frightened out of their lives. There was an inquiry into it by the government and one of the civil rights leaders led the delegation over to London to meet Lord Somebody or other.

Anyway, my bould Dicky went with them as a witness. He was called to give his account of the night and it went something like this. He could hyphenate any word going with the four-letter word 'fuck': 'I was fucking lying in my fucking bed . . . ' He was stopped short here by the clerk or some fellow trying to make a name for himself but the judge waved him on and told him to proceed in his own words. It was here that Dicky got her into top gear: 'As I was fucking saying, your Honour, before that fucker interrupted, I was fucking lying in my fucking bed and I had a wile fucking sore head when, fuck me, there was this fucking clatter out in the fucking street and next fucking thing the fucking windy came in on fucking top of me. I put my fucking head out and saw a whole fucking crowd of black bastards running up and fucking down the fucking street, fucking battering in the fucking windies and doors. So I says, "Fuck me!" and I fucking dived under the fucking clothes again. They were fucking cursing away, your Honour, and it wasn't very nice.' By this time, the whole company were in howls but his evidence was noted.

Poor Dicky died a couple of years later and I recall meeting a gypsy some time ago who asked me if I knew Dicky and when I said I did, his eyes lit up and he pulled himself up straight and said, 'He was a prince.' I said that I agreed and then in the next breath he says. 'He was smart. Do you know, he could tell you there was 240 pence in a pound?' It doesn't matter who you are, there is someone in the world who will think you're wonderful. It taught me a good lesson that day. I pray for Dicky every day. God rest him.

I can't pass Dicky without a mention of a character we'll call the Big Fella, though he was also known in those days as Jim Figgerty, the man who put the figs in the fig rolls. This was from an ad running on television at the time and the star in it was a dead ringer for the Big Fella, a big man with a walrus moustache. He too could use the four-letter word. Agnes used to be afraid to meet him, which at times couldn't be helped, for, as I said, with the civil rights you would find yourself mixing with strangers. After a conversation with him you had really to concentrate on what you were saying, as he used the four-letter word so much, some of it was bound to stick. By the way, it was Agnes christened him Jim Figgerty and it stuck. He claims the first time he heard the four-letter word was when the police gathered outside his house during the battle of the high flats and the Bogside.

This was when the young people took things into their own hands and declared a block of flats about ten storeys high as their own. The account is well-documented so I won't go into the mechanics of it, save to say that it lasted a number of days and try as they would to recapture the flats the police were at a standstill. I had occasion to be over in the district every morning picking up fish and had a ringside seat. The police were lying all round the junction of Rossville Street and William Street, really looking the worse for wear, and the sergeant would try to rally his men to get up and at them. The poor fellows had

had it all night and then some wag from the top of the flats would start with a loud hailer: 'Good morning, campers, I do hope you had a good night's sleep. Well, we have a lovely breakfast ready, but first a shower...' and with that a fire hose would be turned on and all the police soaked.

Sometimes I think it was a mistake that the young lads won that battle – mind you, it's only my opinion – for when the army came in and the lads came down on their own I think they felt victorious. It wasn't so long after that they took on the British Army, which is still here, somewhere. Trust was a victim, too, for strangers were given a wide berth in case they were detectives. Not that you had anything to hide but there was no sense in speaking to the enemy! I remember a fellow used to bid me the time of day in the street and I would do my best to ignore him, thinking he was a detective trying to get in with me for information. Information? Me? It was completely out of character for me to ignore anybody, so one day in Andy Hinds's papershop the guy spoke to me again. After he went out I says to Andy, 'Who's your man?' and Andy says, 'That's Mickey Gillen, the teacher. Do you not know him?' I was so relieved that I almost followed him out of the shop just to start up conversation with him. He must have thought me a rare duck, for the next time we met I was all over him with the chat.

Back to the Big Fella. He was a great one for getting into the limelight and Derry was big news back from '68 through '74 and during this time a part of Derry became a no-go area for the police and the army. It became known as Free Derry. Some of the men started to police it themselves and amongst them was a fellow called Alex Hegarty who took up point duty at the intersection – that's American – of Rossville Street and William Street and a good job he did too. The Big Fella got wind that a television crew was making its way over from the City Hotel to record this guy. He ran like the clappers – big gut and all –

to his house on the corner of Rossville Street, told his wife to make the tea, nipped out to Alex and said, 'The wife wants you over for a cup of tea. I'll hold the fort till you come back; so away you go now and take your time.' No sooner had Alex gone than the television crew arrived and now the Big Fella is recorded on tape for posterity. It goes to show that you can't really believe all you see in the papers or television after all.

These are lessons you learn from the University of the Street. Needless to say, as soon as the television crew left, the Big Fella sent word over to the house to see what was keeping poor Alex. Alex's son was shot a short time afterwards when the army decided they had had enough of Free Derry and moved in in force, one morning just before daybreak, calling it Operation Motorman. It would take a book on its own to cover some of the days we had at that time. The Big Fella also featured in the day of the Burntollet affair when we got ambushed at loyalist Irish Street and he, like myself, was only there to keep the peace. This old biddy attacked him, so he thumped her one and a cop arrested him for assault. Out of all the stoning and beatings the marchers got that day his was the only arrest.

The Big Fella was credited with saying to some of the young stone-throwers outside his house one night, 'Don't corrugate round that lamppost, boys, for you'll be sitting targets for the police.' I remember once the man who came to our house to read the electricity meter was having a wee cup of tea with Agnes and me and somehow the conversation came round to the Big Fella. He said, 'Do you know him? The big bastard had the whole street up last night batin' binlids because an army patrol was passing by and he went on to his bed while everybody was out in the street.'

The Burntollet incident was another day of infamy in the civil rights campaign, for a group of students calling themselves People's Democracy, led by, among others, Bernadette Devlin

215

– at one time the youngest elected MP in the British parliament – set off from Belfast to march to Derry. As they were passing through the various wee towns they came under some severe harassment, under the ever watchful eye of the RUC. It took a couple of days, for the distance was about a hundred miles and their progress was monitored hourly in the radio and in the newspapers. The final crunch came as they approached Burntollet Bridge about six miles from Derry where the loyalists, all good normal churchgoing citizens, laid an ambush and attacked the young students with everything they had, short of guns. They used pickhandles with nails in them and clubs; some even tried to drown the students in the river and all this time the RUC turned their backs. This is where we joined them from Derry. We did not give them our full blessing on the march but now that it was started we couldn't stand by to see them battered and abused. We were too late, for a lot of the youngsters were already in the hospital.

We escorted the rest of the marchers into Derry and ran into another ambush at Irish Street and again the RUC turned their backs to the loyalists and 'saw nothing'. This too is well-documented, so I won't labour it too much, only to say that the chief steward and myself had a disagreement about the route. When we reached Spencer Road there was another shower of stones from the quarry above us. Having been born and reared in the district, I knew where the next attack was coming from, so I tried to warn him but he wouldn't listen. The loyalists were standing on high ground above the road we had to pass and once again a shower of rocks came down on top of us like hailstones. It was frightening; no quarter was shown to this peaceful march. Meanwhile the policemen again turned their backs, as they had done at Burntollet.

One day Agnes and myself were doing the usual run in the fish and chip van near Burntollet Bridge. When the time came to move off, I heard a clanking at the back of the van and I got out thinking it was kids hanging on. There was a length of tongue-and-groove board hanging on the back; it read: 'Red Doran, John Hume's Man'. I ripped the board off and said to Agnes, 'This is the last time we'll be coming here.' And so it was, for very shortly after at 2 am on 5 October 1972 we got the message loud and clear.

I was doing so well with the van that I had moved from our three-bedroom bungalow to a big four-bedroom house, one of four just privately built. At the time I should have had more sense, for it was in a Protestant area. But then, why would any-one harm me? I was so well-known and, I might add, respected. Well, all I can say is that there are over 3,000 people in the graveyards all over Northern Ireland who probably said something similar. At 2 am on 5 October 1972 we were awakened by the crash of glass and the roaring of the hoods out-side. They sounded like redskins round a wagon train in the movies, shouting, hollering and stoning the windows. The at-tack lasted about three minutes – remember, I used to box three-minute rounds – and then they went up the drive, making plenty of noise as they went – no fear in these lads.

The house was a wee bit lower than the road, so that when they got into the car they had a good clear shot at the door. During the attack my thoughts were about the safety of the weans upstairs but as Agnes and myself slept downstairs I was jammed in the hallway and couldn't get up because of the deluge of glass and stones coming down the stairs. We had big dormer windows that ran all the length of the roof, from one bedroom across the landing to another bedroom, and as it was a safe bet that we were all in bed, these were the first windows to go. The children were terrified; it was a crime to waken them up in that manner at that hour of the morning. It was bedlam! All hell was let loose but nobody attempted to come in through the front door, which was 80 per cent glass. I had thrown Agnes out of the bed, but with these modern low beds – give me an Isle of Doagh bed any day – she couldn't get under it. She had to be content to pull the clothes over her head. What I didn't know was, they were up on the windowsill throwing stones in at her and laughing at her pleading to the Blessed Virgin to save her. I would say they got good crack out of that.

Meanwhile I was jammed in the hall trying to comfort the children and speaking in a whispered voice, 'Get under the bed; don't look out the windows; stay where you are!' You see, with all the broken glass and stones flying I was afraid the children would either attempt to look out the windows or try to come down to us, their mother and father. It was a hectic three or four minutes but the hullaballoo stopped as quick as it started. I could hear the four doors of the car close and the engine rev up, and this is where the wicked part comes in, for they expected me to run to the door to get a fleeting glimpse of my attackers. I was too busy calling up to the children and saying at the same time to Agnes, 'Don't move! Stay where you are!' when the gun opened up and five bullets, as neat as you like, came through the door. One caught me slightly in the neck and the ear lobe but, as I learned later, they were meant to do a lot more damage. The car then sped off.

The deed was done and I can only say it was a genuine murder attempt. As I've already stated, it was 2 am and pretty dark, and we didn't put on any lights to show ourselves. I got Agnes, took her upstairs through the broken glass and assembled all the weans together and asked if any were cut. They were in a state of shock and I hugged them all together and thanked God. Do you know that that was the best thing I ever did because I never looked for revenge and it didn't stunt my growth.

I left the family and went out the back way across the field to the farmhouse on whose land the houses were built. I knocked at the door and the man of the house put his head out of the window and recognised me. When I told him what had happened he called the police. Instead of the police an ambulance arrived and took the family to hospital and they insisted that I go with them. At 4 am, as I was sitting in a daze wondering what had happened, two detectives came into the hospital and introduced themselves, apologised for not coming sooner as they were called to a pub burning shortly after my episode.

They asked me to come down to the house which was close by. Down we went, and I can tell you it was like a scene out of *Wuthering Heights*, with the rain and the wind blowing through the broken windows. All the windows were broken, some of them six feet by eight feet, and the television set and radiogram, and the usual showcase with the family china all wrecked. In one bedroom alone we lifted thirty-two stones the size of your fist. The detectives were more interested in the gunplay and I was kneeling with one of them in the hallway as he was picking up these slivers of metal, when he whispered out loud to himself. 'Jesus, these boys meant business.' I asked him what he meant and he answered, 'These are special, rubbed down; if they hit you they would disintegrate inside and make a big hole coming out.'

I got no compensation except for paint and glass and we never entered that house again. When passing it, which we do quite often, Agnes will give a sigh, for up until then it was her dream house and all she got out of it was six months. As for me, I just did what the apostles were told to do in the Bible – I 'shook the dust off my feet' and never looked back.

I put the house up for sale but it took the agent six months to sell it and it lay empty all that time. One day the bank told me to get rid of it as I couldn't afford it, for there was no money at all coming in. I was now 'into' the bank for £7,500 and had no means of paying it off. I didn't work all this time because to go out in the van again would have been courting death. I would have made an easy target along the road, for, you see, the van worked to a schedule. I would call at a certain place at a certain time and this did not vary more than a couple of minutes either way. It was child's play to set up an ambush, which in fact was what was done, for the van was burned three months later, though, thank God, no one was hurt.

THE BEE'S KNEES

I must tell you about the house where I'm living at present. It wasn't that I was in the market for a new house, for I had just moved into the dream house where we had had to face death. That was to have been the last move but one Saturday morning when I was over the town and passing by this estate agent's office, I saw a picture in the window of a lovely little cottage with twelve acres of land. Who would not love to be a landowner? (That was nearly a lawnmower!) I stepped into the office, enquired about the asking price, asked if the estate agent would let me see it and off we set in his car to view it. I fell in love with it right away, gave the agent the asking price there and then, landed home with the deeds and in my own mind started to plan right away. I always fancied running a pig farm, so this would be the ideal place, away out of the town with no one to bother me.

Looking back now, I realise that it was a bit selfish of me. I usually took Agnes into all matters, only this time I thought I'd surprise her. A couple of days later I took her and our neighbour Patricia Bevington with her wee girl, Caroline, up to see it. I say up because it is sitting on the sunny side of a hill about 300 feet or 400 feet above the town; it's *up* all right. We drove up a long lane to the yard where the gate was closed. Inside there was the loveliest wee farmhouse you'd ever see, with a tin roof, and built tight into the banking behind it. It was long and just one room deep; in other words, if you came in the front door and crossed to the opposite wall you had walked the width. The rooms all ran in line: small bedroom, living-room, kitchen, bathroom and toilet together, and then the master bedroom. Each room had two long windows and inside each window there stood a mountain of a dog, standing on its back legs against the window frame, barking its head off. The woman of the house was the secretary of the Pyrenean Mountain Dog Club in Derry, and she gave the dogs the run of the house.

It was like a lived-in dog kennel and Agnes and Patricia took physically sick. Do you know, I couldn't blame them, for the stench was awful and the dog hairs were everywhere. To make matters worse, Patricia's wee girl asked to use the toilet. So Agnes took her in, for she was only three and when sitting down, the toilet moved and the wean said to Agnes, 'Aunt Agnes, this seat is moving.' Well, the colour drained from Agnes's face and she checked. The child was right. She was sitting on a bucket. It was a dry toilet. There was no running water and it really was a surprise not only for Agnes but for myself. The price was right, though, and the value has gone up now at least thirty times its purchase price. It was one of my better moves, for six months after I bought it I was wiped out financially. All the big plans I had for it were put to the one side. I had had plans for a new house drawn up and passed and the farmhouse would become a stable for my horses when I got them, with the piggery above. That was all that I'd ever hoped for.

I had the world at my feet and then disaster struck. Oh, the plans of mice and men! The wee house lay derelict for five years. It took that time for Agnes, because of the terrible night, to agree to live outside a town again in isolation. I didn't blame her but I held on to it in the hope that our dreams would one day come true and thank God they did. There were times that money was a real problem, for I paid more court fees than enough for not paying rates on the house that I was shot out of, but there's an old saying, 'You can't take blood out of a stone', although it was tried on me. By the way, just before the disaster I had started to build a piggery above the house at the back and it lay with no roof on it all those years. I pulled my socks up one day and started to put it together. My architect friend, Liam McCaul, drew another set of plans for the piggery and between us both we designed this house we're living in now.

It was a huge success, although it was a hard struggle. I must say, it was a family effort, for Giovanni, Fionnbarr and even Ciaran laboured where they could, and I was fortunate to have two nephews, one an electrician and the other a carpenter, and they worked for practically nothing. Saying that, little else came easy on the site, for when materials were delivered there always seemed to be awkwardnesses and the bricks and slates and even the roof trusses were all dropped far away from the actual building and they then had to be carried to the site. Still, we got it done and I wish we could do it over again, for the greatest blow of all had yet to come and that was Fionnbarr's sudden death.

Nothing matters after that. When my father died I was too young to understand and my mother and Gerard, Mannix, Terry and the older girls took his place. Then Gerard died and whilst I mourned him it was really for my mother, for she was devastated. With an age gap of ten years and you only sixteen it doesn't seem long enough to really build up a closeness, for want of a better word. I was able to get over Gerard's death and get on with life but my mother never did, and now I know why.

I was old enough when Mannix died and we had a great bond. He was single, always there in the house, and I had more years with him. I miss Mannix a lot these days. Gerard and Mannix were like Giovanni and Fionnbarr, with about a year's difference in age. Gerard died at twenty-six years when Mannix was twenty-five. Giovanni was twenty-eight when Fionnbarr died at twenty-seven. Mannix, like Giovanni, lived on and although they didn't talk of their emotions I'm sure they missed their brothers very much. As I got older the stories were always about Gerard and Mannix. They were like twins. It was the same with Giovanni and Fionnbarr. I know that Giovanni lost a lot when Fionnbarr died. The rest of the children did likewise, for they were all very close and shared their lives with each other. I was too busy with my own and Agnes's grief and at the same time tending for Fionnbarr's wife and son Paul that I almost overlooked the rest of the family. Now I can feel, a wee bit anyway, of what my mother went through. This house in a way has become a memorial, for there are too many happy memories built into it and Fionnbarr was part of it.

I said it took us five years to make the move here and during this time we lived at 1 Carnhill, where we were lucky to be 'emergency-housed' after the assassination attempt. Meanwhile, the farmhouse had windows, doors, a roof and the first fittings for plumbing, and one Sunday I came up to check it only to find it was being used by the army. Thinking it might come under attack or, worse still, be booby-trapped, I decided to move in right away and finish the house around us. Boy, it was cold! In the mornings you could write your name or other graffiti on the ice inside the bedroom windows and the bedclothes at your chin were always wet with condensation. I tried to get a mortgage to finish the house but, according to the estate agent, I was on the wrong side of the dividing line – in this case Creggan Road. On the street map of Derry anything to the left of it was considered bandit country, so no money was available. After some shopping around I was lucky to get a financial injection to allow me to pay off the bank which was strangling me and do a wee bit more at the house. It wasn't enough but I carried on.

At this point I would like to tell you a wee story. In my sailing days I used to visit an old couple whose son I met in Australia. Anyway, during the course of my visits the old fellow took to talking to me like a father and he gave me a bit of advice: 'Always have a few pounds in your pocket, for if you see a bargain go for it then. Don't stall or go home to sleep on it, because the seller may sleep on it too and next day it could cost more!' Too true, for it happened to me. I was getting it very tight and the work at the house came to a standstill. There was no money to go any further. I was finished and one day I must have been thinking out loud, I said to the bricklayer, 'I wish some boy with an eye to the trade would buy it off me.' Well, that night two fellows came to my door and asked me if I had a site for sale and I said, 'Yes. But look: I'm not dickering. I owe the bank £7,500 and I can't take a penny less.' They hummed

225

and hawed and said, 'We'll come back', but, thank God, they didn't, for the next week I got the financial injection and did what I did. I finished the house.

The best was yet to come, for the company that gave me the mortgage of £10,000 valued the property at £40,000 and that was for the house only – to think I was giving it away for £7,500! Some time later I decided to get parquet floors and when the tradesman came to measure up he said to me, looking round the house, 'You know something? I need my arse kicked.' 'Why?' said I. 'I could have bought this place and twelve acres of ground for £7,500.' Aye, or even less. That was the key to it all: he was going to dicker and he didn't recognise a bargain when he saw it. He was one of the fellows that came to my house that night in Carnhill when I was at my lowest. End of story.

After the van was burned I was offered a job in St Columb's senior boys' college on the Buncrana Road as canteen supervisor and I took it, as they say in Derry, to get 'in off the streets'. The wages were ministry wages and I realised after a while that I was the only 'man' in Northern Ireland holding this position. Despite all the equality talk it was still a woman's job with a woman's pay. It suited me at the time and Monsignor Coulter, the college president, gave me the tuck shop concession in the Bishop Street school where there were no canteen facilities and I was able to fill the bill. Again Agnes and myself worked hard at lunchtime, serving sweets, sausages and chips, not necessarily in that order, although the wee boys could eat them in any order. With the tuck shop and my job in the canteen, I was able to live. Meantime my own children were at third-level education, Marina and Adian at the Poly, Giovanni and Fionnbarr at the New University of Ulster, and still at secondary school, Siobhán and Ciaran.

The children cost me nothing, for they lived well within

their grants. I don't know how they did it but they did and I'll never forget it. In fact when times got rough they even chipped in, so no credit is due to me there. This is the time to say a loud thanks to them!

I worked for approximately fourteen years in the college and when the Bishop Street tuck shop closed down after about six years I compensated with doing home-catering: christenings, birthday parties, anniversaries, small or large weddings in local halls, even funerals. I was there or rather *we* was there! Agnes was my right arm and helped me no end. It was 'the greatest business to be in', for one party or gathering advertised another and I got to the stage where I had to turn work away. By the way, it was also very tiring, both mentally and physically, so at the time of writing this I have retired.

Once again it would seem it was all me doing things. Well, I'm sorry to give you that impression, for Agnes had a full-time job as well as helping me in my work. Monsignor Coulter came into my office one morning and said, 'John, I'm looking for a woman', and he must have realised what he had said, for he smiled. I ignored it and said, 'Sure, Monsignor, how can I help you?' He replied, 'I'm looking for a woman answerable only to me to take charge of the care of the school. Now it's not a cleaner I'm looking for but a woman to take charge, and I'll leave it up to you.'

I thought this was rather a tall order because he had a personnel officer and a bursar, so why come to me? But whatever his reason, I thought I would look around for him. That night after going through a list of names with Agnes and getting nowhere, I said to her, 'Would you tackle it yourself?' After some coaxing, for she didn't think she was capable, she said, 'OK, if it's all right with Monsignor Coulter.' Next morning I put it to him. He was delighted and gave me a bunch of keys for Agnes for every lock in the building. Poor Agnes, that first day she was afraid to use some of them in case she was offending somebody. The school had been running now for about a year and the existing cleaning staff were working aimlessly under a male caretaker who wasn't cut out for housework. The floors were in a terrible state, so a lot of work had to go into bringing them up to scratch. Agnes loved the challenge and rose to it and she and Monsignor Coulter got on like a house on fire.

Agnes stayed there for ten years but the deaths of Fionnbarr and then Monsignor Coulter took its toll, so she retired with ill health. As for myself, I stayed in the college until retirement and although I had sixteen women in my staff in the kitchen I can safely say I never had a cross word. Any problems amongst ourselves were solved by ourselves in the kitchen. I was the cook supervisor and the buck stopped with me but we were all workers. I enjoyed every minute I was there.

I next tried my hand at beekeeping. That was a howl but I loved it. What beat me and the bees was that I was just too nosy and had to open the hive every dog's turn and check what they were doing. No self-respecting bee likes that, so they swarmed off eventually and left me. I got little honey, as a matter of fact none, but I did get cured of my arthritis by their stings. This is a fact and each year I purposely get stung one way or the other to keep it at bay. Until I joined the beekeepers' association and attended their talks, I never knew there were so many experts and the majority of them seemed to be parish priests or retired reverend gentlemen. All I could hear was, 'Father So-and-so is good at the bees and the Reverend What-you-may-call-him, whatever he doesn't know about them is not in the books.' So everybody was an expert and I became one too. Oh, what a little knowledge can do!

I knew a presenter in Radio Foyle and told him I kept bees, so nothing would do him but he would interview me at the hive. Before I knew it I was on Radio Foyle talking my way through a search of the hive for queen cells and sounding as if I knew my stuff. This life is all a game of bluff, for I met some of my fellow beekeepers after and they congratulated me on the talk. Just goes to show you, eh? There's nothing so daunting, aye, frightening even, for the uninitiated as to witness a swarm of around 40,000 bees in flight looking for a place to light and when they do cluster it's spectacular. It's then they are at their calmest and can be easily handled but the average person doesn't know this, so you get to show off a bit here. Usually when they swarm, they will land on a bush or under the eves of somebody's house and this is where the big show off comes on the scene, like Captain Marvel or in my case 'Red Adair' Doran. The occupant of the house usually panics and calls the council and then I or some other beekeeper would be asked to go and lift the swarm, while everybody stands marvelling at his bravery. At that stage, however, the bees couldn't possibly sting you, as it's a physical impossibility, because when they swarm they are gorged with honey. One of my mental pictures of bees is on a wet or damp day in spring when the hedges and flowers are in full bloom. They don't fly, so I can see them all sitting with their wee arms folded, looking out of the hive entrance wishing the sun would dry everything up so that they could all get out.

PIGGING COWED!

W hen I first bought my present home I had no stock to put on the land and it's surprising how many people approached me to tell me what to do with it. Since I hadn't a clue about farming I knew that growing crops was out of the question. Then along came this wise guy, his name doesn't matter, but by his talk I should have had cattle on that land as soon as I bought it. Well, he gave me such a dressing-down that I apologised for not thinking sooner. I talked to my brother-in-law, Joe, and he agreed to finance the price of six cattle. I got in touch with

Smart Aleck and away he went to the market and bought them. He called them 'kettle', like the country folk did, but I called them cows, for they looked like cows to me. It took a while to sort that out.

I thought the cattle were lovely and they looked so content lying there up to their necks in grass and not a care in the world with the weather so beautiful in early spring. It would have done your heart good to just stand and watch them chewing their cud; but disaster struck again, for your man landed up to my place again (don't forget we hadn't started to live here yet) and he had a bullock with him, which he asked me to put in with mine till he would sell it later. What the hell! I said OK but little did I know that his bullock was a 'discontent'. The grass in this field wasn't good enough for it, so it tried to live up to the old saying 'far off fields . . .' Well, you know the rest of it. Out it went over the hedge, taking my six with it, to roam the country-side at will.

I drove up every day from Carnhill to see them because I was advised this was the thing to do and I would spend hours look-ing for them along the roads and in other people's fields. I was even told how to identify their 'clap' along the road. I was get-ting as good as Cochise at reading signs and at times I was begin-ning to feel a wee bit like the Good Shepherd, for my cows got to know me so well that whenever they went into the Ter-monbacca Home Farm fields and mixed with about fifty or sixty other 'kettle', all I had to do was show my face and they would cut out and follow me. By this time the 'runner' had gone but he left six discontented cattle behind him. Some days only two or three would break out and when I would round them up – I thought I'd never get to use that phrase – the other cattle would gather round them, huddling like American football players and I'm sure they were asking each other how they got on. It was fantastic to watch them. One would skip out of the scrum and off down the field with the others in hot pursuit, like a crowd of young boys getting out of school. I enjoyed every minute of it.

Then came the other side of the picture: all through the summer the cattle grazed and got fatter, although they were too young to sell yet. As the autumn came and the grass got thinner, I realised I hadn't made provision for the winter. I should have had hay left in for them but I was ignorant of this and when Smart Aleck appeared again he gave me a whole litany about what I should be doing. He then proceeded to open the gates and drive the cattle out to graze on the 'long acre' along the road, for free. I felt like a beggar; so one day in the height of a blizzard, as I was rounding-up again, a cattle-dealer-cum-butcher stopped alongside me on the road and asked if I wanted to sell. I said, 'Yes!' and he didn't dicker but gave me my asking price, wrote out a cheque in the car and when I suggested he look at them in daylight he said, 'Don't bother! Leave them where they are!' and drove off. I never saw them again.

Just one wee story before I go off cattle. I was advised to inject them for worms and fluke and whatever else might ail them; so one Saturday, Giovanni, Fionnbarr, Ciaran and myself put all the cattle into a wee outhouse and in we all go armed with the needle and syringe. I saw the vet doing it on television and it looked so easy, and so it was. First I stuck the needle on its own into the cow's rump. (I am being polite; I really should say its arse.) Then I hoped to hook on the syringe but the cow was going through the roof at this stage. They all started to clap at the same time, with their tails swishing back and forwards full of the runniest cowclap you ever did see and it beating us four up the face and all over our clothes. It was crazy. We were cow-clapped literally from head to foot and on top of this we had to drive home. The car was minging and we had to get hosed before we got into the house. You know, that's why I am grateful and very proud of the family I have, because they shared and took part in *everything*. I think we had fun.

Then I tried my hand at pigs. God, they were a squeal (if again you'll forgive the pun). The Christian Brothers whom I swore I would have nothing to do with ever again on leaving school, moved into a mansion a couple of fields from me and since I was classed as a neighbour we somehow got friendly. They had mellowed and I found them a lot more reasonable than in my schooldays. Brother Monds was in charge, with Brother Connolly as his assistant, and we got on like a house on fire. They kept pigs, so it was a natural progression that I would get involved. They picked me out a nice young sow, told me she was mated and would soon produce young piglets, no less. What do you expect? I brought the sow home, we christened her Sue, after a girl on television that the presenter kept calling 'The Lovely Sue', and she was duly installed into a lovely wee pig *cró*. There she never had it so good, with all the food she could eat, her run cleaned out a couple of times a day, spoken to kindly. Why, she was in the lap of luxury and getting fatter by the minute!

After about six months I got talking to a friend of mine, an 'expert' in pigs, and casually asked him what the gestation – he didn't know what the word meant either! – time of the pig was. After listening to me trying to get it across in my own words he thought it best to come and look at the pig himself. Being the expert that he was, he quickly came to the conclusion that the sow was taking a hand out of me and she wasn't 'in pig' at all. I had to get her into the wheelbarrow and down to Brother Monds's boar again. Ciaran was with me in this venture as Giovanni and Fionnbarr were at school and girls don't count in matters like this – too technical. One glorious Saturday afternoon some weeks later Ciaran came running in quite out of breath with excitement to say that the sow was lying up the field under a bush and there were wee pigs everywhere.

The panic was on; we hadn't given that part of it much thought. What to do? What to do? We sent for another 'expert' and he advised us to get a bottle of iron and copper mixture and a syringe, which we did, also a sharp knife and a pair of electrician's pliers. He showed us how to clip their tusks and tails and then inject them with the copper and the iron – and, do you know, every one of them lived. It was a great achievement for two city boys. I was proud of Ciaran, for we finished up with thirteen wee piglets and it was great watching them fighting for a place at the 'natural feeders'. (I'm being polite again!) From that litter we picked out our breeding stock and a year later we had built the herd up to ten sows and a boar.

Disaster struck again: the market dropped, or to make it more Wall Streety, the bottom fell out of the pig trade. It wasn't worthwhile feeding them. We sold out and bought twenty black-faced ewes and a ram, and turned them loose on the land. They did very well but when the winter came we had no feeding for them and as it all had to be bought in, it became too expensive, so we sold out. One thing I will say in the sheeps' favour is, they got rid of the bindweed for us, and we got our money back with a little profit. No wonder farmers always seem to be crying. I sympathise with them now, for, you see, 'I Was There.'

My next venture was geese and ducks and it went something like this. I wanted to do things right, so I went to the agriculture college outside Dungannon and bought four geese and one gander. The expert assured me that that would give me a start, so I took his word for it. The geese were already fattened for killing, so I saved their lives. They were about twenty-five pounds in weight and could barely walk, for they were being force-fed and getting no exercise. I put them into the back of the car and headed the fifty miles home and before the journey's end the car was, as on the day of the cattle-syringing, minging. They cost me £120 and it was pitiful to see them trying to walk but I was assured that after a week or so 'running' – that's a good word; you had to see them, really, to understand – about, that they would slim down. I followed instructions and in the mornings turned the geese loose into the field and it worked! I finished up with four lovely big white Dutch geese and a gander.

The next thing was to let them get on with what I bought them for, breeding, and after a couple of weeks I started to collect the eggs. The only drawback was that I didn't have a clocking hen, so I had to resort to an incubator which I was lucky to get from the lab down at St Columb's College. After doing a bit of reading on the subject I started incubating. The eggs, by now over 200 of them, had to be turned and damped four or five times a day for twenty-eight days to simulate the real thing, for the old goose does this all the time. It was a full-time job and once again I was too nosy. After two weeks I started to lamp them to see inside the egg, not really knowing what I was looking for. That first 200 were a flop, so I looked at the four geese and I looked at the gander and I says, 'My boy, it's four to one against you.' I replaced him with a good old Irish-speaking grey gander and that one proved himself.

It was a bit late in the season, so all I got out of the venture was about thirty geese and they proved to be the dirtiest creatures going, for they messed everywhere and ruined the grass. I was stuck with them, for there was no way that I was going to fatten them up like they did at the agriculture college; it just wasn't natural. In between times I bought sixty ducks specially bred for laying. These wee critters didn't weigh more than a pigeon but they were wee laying machines. It was funny in the morning letting them out, for the number of eggs laid decided what time they got out at. Out of the sixty I would get an average of fifty-eight eggs a day, so that wasn't bad, but I swore if I found out who were the thieves slipping out with their eggs in the morning I would wring their necks. I had a good market for the duck eggs, just couldn't get enough of them, and, believe it or not, I started a fashion round Derry for them.

After two years ducks are laid out, so they have to be replaced. By that time I'd had my fill of them and into the bargain I had adopted (or was it *me* they adopted?) a family of foxes and I swear that old Freddy Fox used to lie up in the piece of high ground, covered with whins, on my land. I can imagine him lying there on his back with his two front legs and paws behind his head and the back legs crossed and him looking down at the yard just waiting for me to let out the ducks and geese in the morning and then turning round to the wife saying, 'What'll it be today, darling? Duck, goose or chicken?' Sure as your word he would nip down in broad daylight and pick himself a fowl of some description. My attitude to all this was 'What the hell! He's entitled to live as well as me', so gradually the stock dwindled until one day Paddy 'Toddler' Gallagher arrived up at the house with another fellow I never met before.

Paddy announced that this fellow was going to buy my ducks. I didn't want to sell the fellow a pig in a poke, so I explained that the ducks were bred only for laying. He was adamant that he would fatten them – maybe he was going to use a bicycle pump, I don't know. I had a wee Shetland pony called Rosie and when he spotted it he says, 'I have a cart that'll fit her. I'll swap you for the ducks.' I jumped at the chance and said, 'Look I'll throw in the geese too!' so he was equally delighted. We smacked each other's hands like they do in the market and the deal was sealed. He said he would call for them in the morning, so I kept them in and when he arrived with a trailer we set about loading them in. First we had to catch them in the barn

236

and they flapped and quacked and screeched and most of all shit all over us and I can tell you it was a howl. I was covered from head to foot – face, hair, clothes and all – with pure unadulterated goose and duck shit, but if you think I was bad, he was worse, for he had to get into his car and travel about ten miles through the town. I pictured him being stopped at an army checkpoint for searching, which was the norm for the times. Agnes hosed me down in the yard and I had to buy a new set of working clothes. So much for the ducks and geese; I was glad to see the back of them.

The family started to graduate, first Marina then Giovanni, Fionnbarr and Adian. Siobhán and Ciaran went to technical college and from there Ciaran went on to agricultural college for a one-year course in animal husbandry. After that he got a job with Siobhán on the construction of the new bridge across the Foyle. The contract lasted almost five years, and then one day it was over. The bridge was built, so they moved on. Siobhán was lucky enough; without any downtime she started in the job she is in at present as a personal secretary and Ciaran moved to Letterkenny, met Rita, got married and now they have a son Rudi – a proper rascal, but a likable rascal. Fionnbarr married Frances and they had a son Paul, and most times he is his father's image but there are times I can see his mother Frances in him. Fionnbarr died before the birth of Paul and nothing really mattered after that: the boxing, the Free State army, the separations at sea, the great times cruising the world, America, Du Pont and even 'the good life' on the farm. A link in the family chain had broken and there was no way to repair it. Adian went to Los Angeles and married Basil and they have two sons, Jonathan and Sebastian Daniel. Giovanni took to teaching in a secondary school and now and again he gets itchy feet and takes himself off on holiday somewhere foreign. I think he is planning to go to Brazil some summer. As for me, well, my travelling days are over and I only have my memories to look back on.

POSTSCRIPT

Now that my story has come to a close I would like to thank first of all my wife Agnes for putting up with me for so long whilst I slipped away to the back room to write this. I did shout an occasional, 'Are you all right there?' hoping she would reply, 'Yes', which she always did. Secondly I am indebted to my daughter Siobhán for the patience and help that she showed when I had a problem with the word processor, which was often. I would like to dedicate this story to my family and my grandchildren, Paul Doran, Jonathan and Sebastian Daniel Antoon, and Rudi Doran, who know so little about me. I hope you enjoy it half as much as I did writing it.